WITH HOPE IN HER HEART

WITH HOPE IN HER HEART

Sport Media

Poem by Sara, aged 13

Kev,
When I wake of a morning
I go to the room where you used to share
And I'm surprised that you're not there.
All that's there is a photo of you
That stares me through and through,
What they did that day wasn't fair,
And we'll never forget you
And those that were there.
The police should be thrown away
To pay the price they have to pay.
When I see the sun shining,
I think of the day
When you went to see Liverpool play
And a part of me was took away,
So walk on Kev lad,
With hope in your heart,
And never forget me,
Coz I'll be sad.

All my love in me forever

Sara
XXXX

For Mum.
With all our love.

Sara, Lena, Finlay, Michael, Grace,
Danny, Chris, Paul and all the family.

x x x

Written by Sara Williams with Dan Kay

Edited by Chris McLoughlin
Production: Chris Brereton
Copyright text: Sara Williams
Published in Great Britain in 2013
Published and produced by: Trinity Mirror Media,
PO Box 48, Old Hall Street, Liverpool L69 3EB.
Managing Director: Ken Rogers
Senior Editor: Steve Hanrahan
Editor: Paul Dove
Senior Art Editor: Rick Cooke
Senior Marketing Executive: Claire Brown
Senior Book Sales Executive: Karen Cadman

Photographic acknowledgements:
Front cover image: Gavin Trafford, Liverpool Echo.
Other images: Sara Williams, Trinity Mirror, PA Pics.

Printed and bound by CPI Group (UK) Ltd, Croydon, CR0 4YY

ISBN: 978-1-908695-17-8

Contents

Foreword by Kenny Dalglish   11

1.   Day Of Truth   15
2.   A Formby Mum   20
3.   Our Kev   31
4.   One Word   49
5.   Long Road   59
6.   A New Approach   81
7.   Heroes   97
8.   Brick Walls   114
9.   From The Heart   128
10.   Two Lives   137
11.   My Red Family   159
12.   Breaking Through   188
13.   Moment Of Truth   216
14.   Time To Say Goodbye   232

What They Say About Anne   255
Timeline: 1951-2013   284

About the co-author:

Sara has written this book with award-winning Liverpool Echo digital journalist and lifelong Liverpudlian Dan Kay who worked with Anne in recent years on her battle for truth and justice.

Since April 1989, the Echo has stood alongside the families and survivors in their quest to put right the wrongs of Hillsborough, and printed a 'Now The Real Truth' front page in response to The Sun's heinous lies just days after the tragedy.

Anne's story first featured on the front page in February 1992 and the paper has followed the campaign right the way through to the ultimate day of truth, September 12 2012, when their contribution was commended in the House of Commons following the publication of the Independent Panel's report.

Everyone associated with the Echo remains totally committed to supporting the families and the survivors for as long as it takes until the justice the 96 deserve is finally achieved.

Foreword:
Kenny Dalglish

ANNE was in so many ways a true heroine in the way she went about trying to correct the wrongs that resulted in the death of her son Kevin.

What struck me especially about Anne was the way she conducted herself down the years with such dignity and humility, such courage and determination.

She tried and fought so hard over so many years to get the result she wanted and believed in, yet I'm sure there must have been many times when she felt it was all going nowhere. But still she never, ever gave up.

Anne kept going and going and eventually she got her wish to have the inquest on her son re-opened.

Kenny Dalglish

Foreword

I met Anne on the day the truth finally came out in September 2012 and the announcement was made by the Prime Minister in the House of Commons.

What I saw that day for myself was her incredible strength of character; her determination in finally getting the breakthrough after fighting the establishment and coming out on top.

That was a huge achievement.

Kenny Dalglish

1

Day Of Truth

*'I'll never forget how she looked that day,
she had a beautiful smile on her face'*

WEDNESDAY, September 12, 2012.

I went into my little boy's room, drew back the
curtains and looked straight up at the sky. I'd been
hoping for nice bright sunshine. It always feels like it'll
be a good day when you see blue skies first thing in the
morning.

It was pretty ordinary-looking, though. Except that
this was no ordinary day. This was the day we'd been
waiting nearly a quarter of a century for.

September 12 had been chosen as the day when the
Hillsborough Independent Panel were at last going to

release their report after taking nearly three years to compile their findings. Back in 2009, the Home Office had finally given in and agreed to the early release of all documents relating to Hillsborough. The power of feeling unleashed at the 20th anniversary had contributed to that. The panel had been given the job of overseeing the release of the information.

So, as morning arrived, we knew that it could be a momentous day. A game-changer.

Outside Anfield, a Liverpool flag was fluttering in the breeze above the Hillsborough memorial. The eternal flame flickered expectantly behind the glass next to the names of the 96, including, of course, 'Kevin Daniel Williams, 15 Years'. My brother.

A few miles away in the city centre, preparations were under way at the Anglican Cathedral, where the documents would be released and the world's press were gathering to analyse them, and St George's Hall, the scene of an evening vigil.

In London, the House of Commons was readying itself for an historic day where politicians of all persuasion would queue up to have their say on the Panel's findings.

2012 is a year that we will always remember, for all sorts of reasons.

It didn't get off to the best of starts. Mum had been poorly for a few months and in January she was diagnosed with a bowel condition. It was a worry, but from her point of view at least she knew what the problem was. The doctor sorted her out with some medication and by the time we went to London for Kevin's debate in February she seemed to be on the mend. She was even able to have a joke about it.

It was around the time of Kev's birthday in May that I started to get more concerned. Mum's condition hadn't improved. In fact, the weight was falling off her and she was in more pain than ever.

Things didn't get any better through the summer. There were constant trips backwards and forwards to the doctors and eventually they sent her into the Countess of Chester Hospital at the end of August. Days went by and the doctors still weren't too sure about exactly what was wrong. She feared that she would be forced to spend September 12 in a hospital bed. That was the last thing any of us wanted after all she had been through. Thankfully, after ten days, she was starting to feel a bit better. The doctors said she could come home on the Monday, just 48 hours before the big day.

Mum had her hair done on the Tuesday and did a couple of interviews at home before travelling to Liverpool to stay overnight as the families had to be at the Anglican Cathedral quite early on Wednesday morning to meet with Bishop James Jones, the Bishop of Liverpool, who was heading up the Panel. The families were due to be told the findings before they were released publicly.

My little boy Finlay had also been counting the sleeps until Wednesday, September 12, 2012, but for a very different reason. It was his fourth birthday.

"Mummy, Mummy, when are we going to see Nanny?" I picked him up, gave him a big kiss and told him, "Nanny loves you very much but she'll have to give you your present a bit later on because today is a big day for her as well."

I can't help but smile whenever I think back to the day we found out the date the Panel's report would be released. We'd been told originally it would be in the spring of 2012, but they ended up having to put it back for some reason. Eventually they sorted it out and Mum was so excited.

"September 12th, Sara," she said. "Finally. I can't wait. I wonder what they're going to say. They best not stitch us up again."

"It's Finlay's birthday that day," I told her. "I won't be able to go."

I may as well have been talking in a foreign language as she just carried on chattering away about the Panel, what they'd been like when she met them and what might happen now.

It was only a few weeks later when she was sorting out the arrangements for who would be going with her on the day that she realised what I'd been trying to tell her.

"Oh my God!" she said. "Why didn't you tell me? It's got to be a good sign that it's Finlay's birthday. Maybe it's an omen. Maybe this time we're finally going to get the truth."

There was a part of me that would have liked to have been in Liverpool with her on that day of days, but it was lovely just having our own little gathering at home and keeping an eye on the TV as the party went on around us, with Finlay running in and out of the garden shouting, "Nanny's on telly, Nanny's on telly."

Early that evening, I glanced at the TV and there was Mum, standing on St George's Plateau, with a beautiful smile on her face.

I don't know if I'll ever get my head around the fact that, just six short weeks later, she was given the news she was dying.

I'll never forget how she looked that day.

After all those knock-backs and all those years, she was proved right in front of the the whole world.

And no-one can ever take that away from her.

2

A Formby Mum

'Too many things happened in her life that weren't fair. She kept an innocence about her'

MUM was one of four kids. The second eldest. 18 months younger than my uncle Danny, two years older than my auntie Pauline and 15 years older than uncle Chris. They were quite a close-knit group even if they didn't always see a lot of each other at certain times.

Whenever they met at family events you could tell straight away how close Mum, Danny and Chris had been, even if they might not have actually spent much time together for months or years beforehand. That bond was always there.

For her brothers, not having Mum around is still hard

to comprehend. They miss her every day. Getting used to the reality that she is no longer here is incredibly difficult. Memories of growing up with her in Formby remain fresh.

Mum was born on February 6, 1951 and from what I've been told was quite a shy, timid girl, although I found that hard to believe when I was growing up! Danny has told me how most children of that time were very naive. I suppose it was a different world back then in the 1950s.

Danny and Mum were both born in Watchard Lane, Formby, where they lived with their parents and grandparents. Their dad – my grandad – was a farm labourer, working long hours and 365 days a year for little pay at Rimmers Farm, which used to be situated opposite Formby police station.

Their grandfather, who they called Pappy, was a merchant seaman during the war and was badly injured as a result of his ship being sunk in the Atlantic.

The conditions they lived in were a world away from what many kids grow up with now. Doctors advised them to move out of Watchard Lane due to the threat of TB and they were put on the 'overspill of Formby' list with 50-plus families before being relocated to Broad Lane, off the old Southport road, opposite Woodvale aerodrome.

There were five separate sites of converted huts used by the RAF during the war and they lived at number

57 on the furthest site. It was a long walk to Our Lady of Compassion primary school in Formby for Mum.

The dwellings on Broad Lane were very basic, being divided to accommodate two families, each having a very small kitchen with one cold water tap, a living room and two bedrooms. The toilet was an elsan bucket, situated outside and emptied weekly.

The only heating was from a coal fire. Mum would recall how it was very cold in winter and icicles would form on the inside of the windows. In bed at night they would struggle to breathe due to having so many army blankets and old coats covering them to keep warm.

Danny told me how it used to be.

"Bath time was a tin bath in front of the fire, the water being heated from the old galvanised boiler with a gas ring, which was also used for washing clothes. There was no form of insulation or sound proofing, if the neighbours had their radio on we would turn ours off.

"Although it was hard for our parents, we didn't know any different and were happy. In the summer, we could wander free in the woods and open fields, there were plenty of other children to play with and lots of wildlife.

"Anne and I were never far from each other, anything I did she would want to do as well. On one occasion I was helping our dad lay a brick path to the outside loo. Anne was trying to help, but was told she would get hurt because the bricks were too heavy.

"To prove us wrong, she picked one up and dropped

it on my head. I am convinced to this day that was the start of my bald patch!"

In 1953 Mum's sister Pauline was born at home and Danny and Mum wanted to know where she'd come from. The nurse told them she'd brought the baby in her little black bag and put her together – a story that they believed for many years!

"The following year, when I started school," Danny continues, "Anne got very upset and cried a lot as she didn't want me to go. I cried a lot too because I didn't want to go either. Then, when Anne started school herself, she cried so much when she got there that they put her in a little chair next to me in my class until she got used to it. That's what big brothers are for."

After many years the family were relocated by the council to Royal Crescent at the other end of Formby. On the day they moved, apparently, they loaded all the belongings, including the kids, onto a tractor and trailer and off they went across the village. They must have looked like war refugees.

I remember Mum telling me how she couldn't believe it when they arrived at their new home because it felt so big, with stairs, a front and back door, hot and cold water, a bathroom and separate toilet. She said she was very excited, but also very nervous.

For many weeks after they moved in, her and Danny were frightened to go upstairs without each other. They just weren't used to having stairs and when you're kids with vivid imaginations you just don't know what might be up there.

Getting used to their new, more comfortable surroundings took some time. Apparently, Mum wouldn't use the flush toilet unless Danny held her hand because she was scared of being flushed away!

As they were one of the first families to move in to the estate, a lot of the houses were still being built so it was like a massive adventure playground for them. You'll play anywhere as a kid and a building site with half-built houses to run in and out of or hide in was an exciting place to be.

Sadly, despite moving to what was luxury compared to what they had been used to, the relationship between my grandparents got worse over the next few years. Mum, Danny and Pauline were caught in the middle of it all and eventually grandad left.

"Mum was very bitter," explains Danny, "and did her best to turn us against our dad, which worked for a while. I regret to say this as we only ever got one side of the story. She even tried to stop us seeing him, without success, thankfully."

It must have been a tough time for Mum and it wasn't helped by an occasionally difficult transition to secondary school. In 1962, when she was 11, she joined Danny at Our Lady of Lourdes Senior School in Birkdale.

"During our time there she was getting bullied by a particularly nasty boy because of her birthmark," continues Danny. "He called her 'Scarface' and other cruel names, but when we reported this to the head-master he told us not to be so sensitive and to stop wasting his time. When the bullying got worse, I couldn't see her upset any more and took the law into my own hands. I was severely punished, but it was worth it as the bullying stopped.

"Even so, Anne found it harder than any of us to accept Dad leaving. It left her very confused and insecure for many years. A lack of understanding in her teenage years didn't help."

In 1965 my grandmother remarried to Fred. He was a happy-go-lucky man and looked after the family well. Danny says he was more like a mate than a step-father.

The following year grandma and Fred had a son, Chris, who they all loved dearly.

Around this time Mum left school and started work as a secretary in the offices of various companies. She got married to her first husband in August 1970, and the following year had Michael, with Kevin arriving two years later.

But although she had two lovely boys, things weren't as rosy for Mum as they might have appeared.

"Anne lived in Cable Street in a property that was really unfit for habitation," explains Danny. "It was damp and infested with mice. Her husband beat her regularly and was also cruel to the boys.

"Anne confided in Mum about the issues she was having to endure, but she gave her no support at all. Cruelly, she turned her away. By this time I was married with two children and living in Birkdale. I didn't know any of this was going on. You can imagine the anger and frustration I felt − and still do to this day − when I found out how my sister had been treated.

"Anne eventually admitted what had been going on to her doctor, who compiled a report. It was eventually used in court to gain a divorce on the grounds of cruelty in 1975."

To make ends meet, Mum worked behind the bar at The Bay Horse and The Grapes Hotel. She enjoyed working in both the pubs as she was able to meet people and it boosted her self-esteem.

It was while working at The Grapes that she met my father, Steve Williams, and they married in 1977. At last, things were working out now for Mum and the boys. She was happy, in a good stable relationship and in July 1979, I was born.

"Anne was such a kind-hearted person," says Danny. "She helped Steve's father through the illness he had and would always try to help anyone in need such as their neighbour, John, who had lost both of his legs. She would cook meals for him, as well as doing his washing and taking him out in his wheelchair. Anne had a heart of gold and would give you her last penny if she thought you needed it."

Danny and my uncle Chris – Mum's other brother – have always been very close, so much so that they have worked together in their own construction business for as long as I can remember.

Chris was thirteen years younger than Mum, though, and has often said that when he was growing up she was more like a Mum to him than a sister. He would spend a lot of time at our house when he was a lad and Mum would look after him along with all of us.

"One of my first real memories of Anne was at her house in Cable Street," recalls Chris. "It was a big old house by the fire station. I would only have been about four.

"I was knocking around in the back room and my Mum and Anne were in the kitchen at the front. Whenever the fire engines were called to go out and attend somewhere there would be a loud noise that went off, much like an air raid siren.

"When it happened on this occasion I was petrified and ran back into the kitchen, straight to Anne rather than my own mother!"

Mum and Chris were very close and had a very strong connection, even though there were long spells when they didn't see each other because of various family fall-outs. Things seemed to settle down by the time Chris was 15 or 16 and he often used to come over to babysit.

He would also come to stay if his grandma and Fred

went on holiday, and, with my dad being away a lot working on the rigs, Chris would be the man of the house – which he loved!

We've got massively happy memories of those times because Mum used to look after us all fantastically well.

When I was little, Chris would even sag off work once or twice and Mum would keep the boys off school for a day. Then it would be party time!

She believed in living life for the moment and we would have some lovely days down by the beach or going into Southport. Years later, Mum would often talk about them, saying, "For the sake of a telling off or a detention it was worth it as long as we'd had a great day. And we always did."

When Chris stayed over at ours he would share a room upstairs with the boys, Kevin in his cot and the two older lads in the bunk beds. Chris and Mike would gather every soft toy and teddy bear they could find onto the top bunk and throw them all into Kevin's cot until he was covered in them. He would be trying to chuck them back at them but couldn't reach.

Mike would run down the ladder, throw them across to Chris, run back up and then bomb poor little Kev all over again!

"I remember Kevin when he was a baby," smiles Chris. "Anne had to put him in the highchair most of the time because he'd always be wandering off so that was the only way she could keep an eye on him.

"One time he was sitting in his chair with this little vest on that was too small for him and started doing this really funny, gruff laugh over and over again. Anne was in hysterics and so were me and Michael. The more he did it, the more we laughed.

"Sara's little boy Finlay is very similar to Kevin in character. Very loveable, a little old man at times, often on the wind-up and a real livewire.

"Anne was very independent and she had to be because she got very little family backing, unfortunately.

"Long before Hillsborough, when I was about 14, my Grandma on my dad's side, Ethel, or 'Granny Eccles' as Anne used to call her, passed away.

"It was during one of those times when many of the family weren't speaking to her. Ethel lived with her brother and sister, and Anne used to see a lot of them around Formby village.

"They all thought the world of her, but there was no place for Anne when Ethel died.

"She wasn't invited to the funeral and I remember sitting in the funeral car about to leave for the burial when Anne came out of the church, having gone anyway to pay her respects.

"My mother saw her and said 'What's she doing here?' Poor Anne was caught like a rabbit in the headlights. She'd done nothing wrong and didn't deserve to be isolated like that.

"From that point on I started to think about everything in a completely different way. Too many things happened in her life that weren't fair, but I've never met anyone like her.

"She had a very dry sense of humour, which she needed, but still kept that innocence about her."

3

Our Kev

*'He was trying to get someone to get him
a ticket. He said 'don't tell me Dad''*

ONE of my first memories of Kevin is when he first
started going to school. I used to start screaming because I didn't want him to go! He started off only going
in on half days but, even for that short time, I didn't
like it when we were apart.

When I started at Freshfield Juniors he would come
over and see me at break time to make sure that I was
okay. I didn't like the skin on my apple, so he used to
peel it off with his teeth and give it me back. He was
always looking out for me, always helping me, and it
was comforting to know.

Maybe I got on his nerves a little bit as, with there being six years between us, I used to follow him around everywhere.

He liked bringing his mates back to our house when our mum and dad were out on a Saturday night so they could smuggle a few drinks in and have a party. I would sneak downstairs and hide behind the sofa thinking I was dead clever, but he always knew I was there.

However, Kevin soon realised that the more attention I got – his girl friends would be going 'Ahh isn't your sister cute' – the more attention he would get so I think he was quite pleased I was there really.

Kevin had this mole on his face that looked like someone had drawn it on with a pen. I drew one on my face once and went downstairs to show it off. His friends thought it was hilarious, saying 'She's got a little brown freckle just like you!' but Kev went mad. "That's felt tip!" he shouted.

My Mum always said she thought I looked like him, although I don't think I do.

I got into football because Kev loved it so much. We would spend hours and hours in the back garden. Most of the time I'd just get shoved in goal and battered with the ball, but he taught me how to kick properly and dribble really well. I was a pretty decent player after his coaching!

I used to play for the girls' team at school, imagining I was John Barnes legging it down the wing, and he'd

always want to know how I'd got on and get me to describe my goals to him when I scored.

And so, because he was a massive Liverpool supporter, I became a massive Liverpool supporter too.

You couldn't talk to Kev if the match was on. There
weren't many games on the telly in those days, but he'd
listen to them all on the radio.

I'd have to sit there in silence because he was con-
centrating on the game. If I started chattering to him,
especially if they were losing, I'd get shouted at and
kicked out of the room!

He didn't mind listening to Genesis with me, though.

Kev really was crazy about them. He liked Pink Floyd
and John Lennon as well, but most of the time he would
be listening to Genesis over and over again.

I liked them too, and still do, especially 'Me and Sarah
Jane' off their Abacab album. Me and Kev would always dance around together to that one and he would
call me 'mop head'. It meant a lot to Mum when Kev's
friends told her that his favourite song was 'Mama'.

She would listen to that album, just called 'Genesis',
all the time. Kevin had only bought it the Christmas
before to add to what he called 'our collection', as he
knew Mum loved the band, particularly their early stuff
with Peter Gabriel. That opening track and 'Home By
The Sea', which she said reminded her of Formby,
were her favourites.

Esther, who was Kevin's girlfriend at school for a

while and has been such a good friend to Mum and me over the years, said how they were studying together one time and she was having a bit of a moan about having to listen to Genesis yet again. She asked him, "Don't you ever listen to anything else?" and he said, "No, and when I die they'll play Genesis at my funeral."

So we did.

Kev was quite protective of me and made sure I knew from an early age how to stick up for myself if anyone thought they could try and pick on me at school. But he was very bright and so hard-working as well. He always did really well at his studies.

I remember him teaching me how to count and we'd always sit together doing our homework at the kitchen table. I felt dead grown up watching him while he was beavering away over his GCSE work while I did my primary school stuff, which was a joke in comparison really, but he'd usually find time to help me if I asked him.

He'd tolerate me most of the time although occasionally he'd lose his rag if I was pestering him too much and go "Right, Sara, out!"

I sat with him the whole time he did his drawing of the European Cup for his art GCSE. He had loads of little copies of it and it took him ages to get it how he wanted. 'Rome 77' he wrote on the top and had Tommy Smith raising the European Cup aloft *(right)*.

To me, it seems like the picture was done ages before he died, but maybe that's just because he took so long over it.

I tried to draw something similar but it was nowhere near as good.

It's only when I look at the date on the picture – April 6, 1989 – that it really hits home that it was one of the last pieces of schoolwork Kev ever did.

One of Kev's best mates at Formby High was Ian Barnes. They were in registration together and would play football at break-time – morning and afternoon – and of a lunchtime, too.

Ian was devastated when Kev died at Hillsborough and has been very supportive to the family. Many years after their school days he became a founder member and a trustee of Hope for Hillsborough, Mum's justice campaigning group.

"I was in the same year at Formby High as Kevin and our form tutor was a big Glaswegian fella called Mr McGrath who had a big handlebar moustache and took no messing whatsoever," recalls Ian.

"The first thing I really remember about Kev was playing football at break time. It was usually quite competitive, and there'd always be people playing in all three slots, first break, dinner time and afternoon break.

"Some lads, if they had won in the morning or at lunchtime, wouldn't turn up for the last one. Never

Kev, though. He would always be there no matter what. He just loved playing footy. And he always had his shoelaces undone and his shirt hanging out!

"One of my fondest memories is of the time we went away on a school trip. It was my first time abroad and we went on the coach to Hull then got the ferry to Zeebrugge. It was only a year or so after the disaster there, which was a bit weird.

"We travelled through Belgium and stopped off at this remote little village in Austria. The teachers knew we'd all be wanting to try and get a bevvy, we'd already managed to sneak a couple on the ferry, so they told us to stay in the hotel with them and we could all have one with our meal.

"It was literally one though and after that it was back up to the rooms while they stood guard at the bar so we had to get our thinking caps on.

"We ended up creating a human ladder out of the window, with one person lowering themselves down then someone else dangling onto them and so on.

"I think it was Paul Johnson who had hold of me, and then I had hold of Kev and in the end it was a lad called Chris Healy who climbed down and ran to the offy. He must have bought virtually all the alcohol in there because people were throwing up by the end of the night!"

Kevin had a great time on that trip. He didn't stop going on about it. I was dead jealous. They went to

Austria, Germany and Italy and he was very proud about the fact that Genesis was the soundtrack for virtually the entire time thanks to his influence.

This was way before iPods and the like, even Walkmans weren't that commonplace, so everyone had to listen to whatever was playing on the coach's tape cassette player.

There was a girl in his year called Kaiye Linaker who was from Australia and was as obsessed with INXS as Kev was with Genesis, so the arguments those two used to get into over whose music would be played were unbelievable by all accounts.

Kev was determined to get his tapes on whenever possible and he was chuffed that by the end of the trip everybody was word perfect on the Genesis tunes, although they were probably sick to death of them by that stage!

Kevin and Ian went to a couple of Liverpool matches together as well, but it wasn't like now when you have to order tickets weeks in advance and join the membership scheme. Most of the time you could just decide on the morning of the game if you fancied going.

Of course you still had to get tickets for the big cup games and derbies ahead of time and there was one occasion when they bunked off school to go to Anfield and queue up.

"We're standing there and who should turn up but our games teacher, Mr Hall," said Ian.

"Our hearts sank as he wandered over to us and we thought about the trouble we were going to be in but he let on to us. 'Alright lads,' he said. 'Here for tickets?' Then he just got in the queue with us!

"He even drove us back to school after we had all bought our tickets, with us still petrified over what might happen, but nothing was ever said. There was just that mutual respect that we were all there for the same reason."

Kevin had a right cob on when he was told he couldn't go to Hillsborough for that FA Cup semi-final in 1989.

I remember him talking with his mate Andy Duncan a few days beforehand as he was trying to get someone to get him a ticket. It was all very last minute. I was earwigging as usual and he said "don't tell me dad."

As soon as he came downstairs on the Friday night I knew he was going to ask if he could go to the match. His face fell when Dad said no. He tried to make out he wasn't that upset, but I could tell that he was. He went back upstairs and slammed the door.

Mum and Dad looked at each other because he'd hardly left the kitchen table, apart from to go to school and his little job clearing glasses in the Bay Horse pub, and they knew how hard he was working and how much he loved Liverpool.

So Dad shouted him back down and said he could go as long as he went with the police escort. He was straight on the phone to Andy, he had obviously already got the ticket. I always wonder where that ticket would have gone if Kev hadn't gone to Sheffield in the end.

I was made up for him. The Reds were on an amazing run of form and it looked like they were going to do the Double again. He was so excited that the first away game he was going to with his mates would be such a big match – the FA Cup semi-final. I couldn't wait to hear about it from him when he got home.

Kev woke up really early to make sure he didn't miss the train so I got up as well to help him get ready. I waved him off at the window and he gave me a cheeky little v-sign as he went off to see Mum in the newsagents where she was working to get bags of crisps for the journey to Sheffield.

That was the last time I ever saw him.

It was a weird day, weather-wise. Warm and sunny, but then cold all of a sudden as well. You don't normally feel it as a kid, but I must have changed clothes a couple of times from trackies to shorts and back again.

Mum had friends who had been travelling in Australia and they were due to be coming around for dinner that night so she was busy cooking, cleaning and washing her hair. I was that bored I ended up picking all the daisies off our front lawn, every single one of them, and put them upstairs in a bag to show Kev when he got home.

Then I just remember it all unfolding on the television. Mum, with her hair still wet because her dryer wasn't working, sitting in front of it on Grandstand with me and my dad and none of us really understanding what was going on.

It wasn't that unusual to see a pitch invasion during the eighties and that's what we thought it was at first. I used to think they were quite exciting. We were sitting there watching it and I remember my dad saying, "If I see our Kevin on that pitch, it'll be the last match he ever goes to anywhere, never mind another away one."

But then they started to say there were people dead.

Seven was the first number they came up with. Then it was 21.

Mum went upstairs to get dressed as she was going to nip down to the Legion to get ciggies and see if anyone down there knew anything. I told her how many dead the telly was now saying and she lost her rag with me a little bit. "Our Kevin's there, Sara," she shouted. It was a very stressful time.

She must have been in a state of pure panic by this point. And, by the time she'd got from where the house was to the top of the road, the number of deaths had gone up to 56. When she got to the Legion it was 73.

We knew Michael would be in there, having a drink and watching the scores as they came in. She came back not long after, if anything in a worse state.

Everyone was in the dark there as much as we were. I knew she was trying to be brave in front of me, but it was written all over her face how worried she was.

Mum's friends Bill and Ian came over for dinner as planned. They didn't have a clue what was going on. Nobody felt like eating, but they just sat around drinking and talking. And waiting. I was just hovering around by this point. I didn't really understand what was happening, but I knew it wasn't good.

They were just sat trying to get through on the helplines all night, feeling helpless. Mum ended up ringing the local police station and they gave her the numbers of the Sheffield hospitals. She rang them all but couldn't get any information about Kev.

Andy Duncan's dad rang to say that he was about to go and pick him up from Southport Infirmary as those with milder injuries had been sent to local hospitals to get treated there. He told us Andy had said that he got separated from Kevin on the terrace in one of the big surges of people. He had tried to go back and find him when he got out, but the police led him away.

Now we knew Kev had been in the middle of it.

Mum suddenly remembered the horn of life chain that Kev wore around his neck, his Christmas present from the year before. It was the early hours of Sunday morning by this stage and she rang the helplines again. This time she got through to someone who said the police would be with us shortly.

That could only mean one thing, although I was too young to realise it at the time.

Nothing happened for ages. The phone didn't ring so Mum and dad decided they had to go to Sheffield to see what was happening. My dad's sister Penny, who had taken us to Anfield the one time Kev and I had been to the match together, raced round to drive them while my grandma came over to look after me.

I remember just hanging about with my mates the next day wondering what was going on. When you're a kid you don't realise. You think it's all just a bit of a game. I saw Andy, Kevin's friend who he'd been at the match with and who was back home by that stage, at the top of the road. He came over and asked me if Kev was back yet. I told him that my parents had gone off to Sheffield to look for him.

It was late afternoon that I finally found out. Auntie Penny phoned to tell my grandma.

I was outside by the front gate. She was alright, my grandma, but she couldn't really handle situations like that very well. She came out of the house and said simply, "I'm sorry Sara, Kevin's died." I just ran off.

I was back by the time Mum and Dad got home. Lots of the family had come around, Mum's mum and dad, my uncle Danny and auntie Pauline. There were lots of tears. I'd never seen so many grown-ups crying. No-one could believe it. It was like a nightmare that we weren't able to wake up from.

I spent most of the next few days at my grans' and uncles' houses. I went with my uncle Chris to the funeral home to see Kevin when he arrived back on the Wednesday. He was buried on the Friday.

We were advised to have the funeral done as soon as possible. Nobody thought anything of it at the time, but as I got older, and saw friends and family sometimes have to wait two or even three weeks to bury their loved ones, it began to strike me as strange that Kevin's was done so quickly.

It's hard now not to feel that the authorities just wanted all the Liverpool fans who died at Hillsborough in the ground as soon as possible. You could say they wanted to bury the evidence.

Not long afterwards we had Kev's ashes scattered at Anfield, just to the left-hand-side of the goal at the Kop end.

I'd only just gone back into school. I'd been absent for a week before everything happened as I'd had bronchitis and then I didn't go in for another week after my brother died. Before my first day back, I thought I was going mad because I couldn't find my packed lunch box anywhere. I asked my dad where it was and he told me that Kev had taken it to the match, as Andy Duncan later told us, so he had something to stand on. I'd noticed when we were at Anfield that Kev's ashes were in this smart black container with his name on in gold letters. I asked afterwards if I could use it for my lunch-box, but my Auntie Penny had already got rid of it.

I'd have used it for that too. It might sound a bit morbid to some people but it was very important to me to keep hold of stuff that had a link to Kev.

I wore his old school tie right throughout my time at Formby High. I took his big red blanket and had that on my bed for years. I wouldn't let my Mum wash it because it smelled of him. I've still got it now. I even painted my room in a vivid Liverpool red which Mum hated, but I loved, for a while.

It's why I probably got even more into football after Hillsborough. I know some people went the other way and wanted nothing whatsoever to do with the game any more. But watching Liverpool makes me feel closer to him. It didn't matter what else was going on, what kind of mood he was in. If the Reds were playing, everything would stop and nothing else mattered for the next 90 minutes.

For a while afterwards my dad was very overprotective of me, inevitably I suppose after what had happened to Kev. I wasn't even allowed to go into Liverpool on the train. But when I left school I started to go to a few matches on my own and, the way football has gone, virtually every match is on TV nowadays or on a big screen in the pub. It means I'm always able to see how Liverpool are getting on and that's important to me because it was so important to Kev.

I always think of him when the Reds win a big match and how happy he would have been with the result. It's impossible not to.

I went through a spell not long after Hillsborough when I thought that what happened to Kev was going to happen to me. Not necessarily that I'd get crushed to death at a football match, just that I might die.

Kev had, out of nowhere, so maybe I would too.

I was lethargic. Miserable. Neurotic over everything, deciding that every time I felt some tiny little ailment it was the beginning of the end. I had a lump in my throat so convinced myself that I must have throat cancer. I had a sore back so that meant there was something badly wrong there that would kill me.

It must have been a big worry to Mum, but she tried to keep things as normal as possible for me. She did take me to the doctors a couple of times but, after asking a load of questions, they could tell it was just a psychological reaction to losing Kev.

It just shows the funny things your brain can do to you, though, because I certainly remember having those backaches and how they felt.

I came out of that phase gradually, but Mum was still going through a really bad time.

There were days when she just couldn't get out of bed and I had to plead with her to get up. She would, in the end, but she was like a shell of herself at times.

People generally were very kind after Kev died. They tried to help out where they could.

All the kids in Kev's year at Formby High dedicated a wall to him which they wrote on and hung drawings and poems upon, while the teachers made a lovely little garden in front of the main school building with his name on a small piece of granite.

It came from the same batch as the Hillsborough memorial at the Anglican Cathedral in Liverpool because the man who made it had a son at the school.

There was a concert at the British Legion to raise funds for the families of the three Formby boys that had died and then there was the Kevin Williams Cup, which was a football match between the teachers and the students that still gets played today.

Even people from as far away as Jersey wanted to help. A group of them, including Mum's cousin Lawrence, raised money to bring some Hillsborough families over for a holiday so mum and dad went there for a week.

I think it did them good to get away for a bit, but I was so happy when they were back. I bought Mum a little furry hedgehog toy as a welcome home present which she put on the hearth.

But nothing was the same without Kev there. On Christmas Day we went to his garden at the school to lay flowers in the morning when we should have been watching him open his presents.

Mum and Dad tried to put a brave face on it for me and Michael, but everyone's eyes kept being drawn to the empty space at the table while we were trying to eat our turkey. It's family times like Christmas when such things can really hit home. So too can anniversaries.

We were all dreading the first anniversary as it drew near in 1990. It didn't seem like anyone in our house actually wanted to attend the memorial service at Anfield, but I did, very much so. We all went in the end, as a family.

It was freezing, even though it was April. We all just sat there crying, unable to believe it had been a whole year since Kevin had gone to watch Liverpool in Sheffield and not come home. It seemed like the agony of his loss was slowly turning into a dull ache that would cast a shadow over our lives forever.

But Mum was about to be given one piece of information that would transform that pain into a burning desire to find out what really happened to Kev.

A discovery that launched her on a personal crusade to get justice for Kevin and the 95 others that lost their lives at Hillsborough.

4

One Word

*'You didn't look like that, Kevin. You looked
lovely when I said goodbye to you'*

MUM always felt that telling the truth about Hillsborough was a form of justice in itself. For many years, that was as close as she was allowed to get.

She was convinced, most of the time anyway, that one day everything would come out, but often said no-one would believe what she'd been through if she didn't write it down.

So she did. I wouldn't call it a diary or a journal, as such, because there was no great order to it. It was more a case of her recording notes and thoughts on an irregular basis.

She'd go months or even years without doing anything and then, all of a sudden, would get right back into again. I would see her sitting there at the kitchen table with her old typewriter, or in later years her laptop, and ask her what she was writing? She would just say, "Oh you know, this and that."

She'd let me take a look at it sometimes and it would be about all kinds. Things from the past. Things that had just happened. Things that might happen. Poems, sometimes.

It was almost like a form of therapy for her, I think. To get things down in black and white helped stop them rattling around her head all the time. Allowed her to switch off from Hillsborough and the fight for justice a little.

I didn't realise how much she'd done until we were clearing out her flat. Getting her first book published meant a lot to her and she said in the last few years how she would like to do another one if she got the chance.

That's why, as a family, we feel it is so important to tell her story now. She was always very keen to take any opportunity she could find to have her say and get her message across. Even in her last few weeks she was still writing things down and talking to her friends in the media. She wanted as many people as possible to know about the fight for justice and I have no doubt that had she lived a bit longer, she would have tried to get another book out. This book.

She kept all her Hillsborough documents and papers organised together so it wasn't difficult for us to find the stuff she had been writing.

Some of her notes go way back. One of the first passages we found was about South Yorkshire Police. They were three words that, over the years, became like a red rag to a bull for Mum.

She ended up on what felt at times like a one-woman crusade to tell the world what they had done to Kev. And it all began when, just for once, they let honesty get the better of them.

Reading Mum's words back, I can imagine the anger and pain she felt while typing them out and how it spurred her on to fight for justice for Kevin, no matter what obstacles were placed in her path.

Mum's words...

It was at Kevin's mini-inquest, just a couple of weeks after the first anniversary, that they let the cat out of the bag.

My solicitor at the time, Mr Farley, had told us we didn't need to go to Sheffield as there would be nothing said that I didn't already know about Kevin's death. These hearings were being held for each of the 96 victims to determine the facts before the main inquest itself, which was due to begin the following year.

But, even though I was dreading it, there was no

way I wasn't going to go. So a year and 17 days after our last trip there, off we went to Sheffield again, on Wednesday May 2, 1990.

Steve and I were driven there by Bob Jones, a social worker who had been assigned to us and had proved to be very helpful, for me anyway, by just letting me talk about Kevin and how I was feeling.

Just before we were due to go into the courtroom, Detective Sergeant John Killoch approached us. He was an investigating officer from West Midlands Police, the force which had been instructed to investigate South Yorkshire's role in the disaster. He had been assigned to Kevin's case and I'd spoken to him on the phone a couple of times.

He took us into a side room and said that he didn't want to cause us any further distress but there was something he felt we should know.

He sat us down and showed us a photograph of Kevin being resuscitated on the pitch by a man in a grey sweatshirt.

I started to cry.

I wasn't prepared for this. They asked me if it was Kevin and I answered yes.

Then somebody who was sat at the end of the desk, I don't know who, took hold of my hand and said that they had something to tell me which would upset me.

They told me that Kevin had been taken into the gym at Hillsborough by a Special WPC, Debra Martin, who said in her statement that just before he had died in her arms at 4pm he had opened his eyes and murmured a word.

I knew straight away what it was.

'Mum'.

I was screaming, "Where is she?" I was told that she would not be there to give evidence but that when we got into the court the pathologists would explain Kevin's injuries to us and we would realise then that it was probably just body wind she had heard.

They added that they were not going to tell me about this but "thought they better had."

I couldn't believe they had chosen this moment to tell me something so significant. I was just about to hear about the last minutes of my son's life and they dropped this bombshell on me. I was given no time whatsoever to take it in.

My mind went straight back to the day it happened. I had had this overwhelming feeling, a mother's instinct, in the British Legion right around the time they were now saying he had called for me, that he wasn't going to come home.

I had told my friend Pat who was there and she had tried to reassure me, but I just knew it in my gut. I remember thinking 'You died then, Kevin...I felt you die'.

I was in a terrible state as we went into the court. The coroner opened Kevin's mini-inquest and just hearing his name made me cry even more.

I was a broken women, I was in bits. I remember looking at the coroner and seeing the jury. I could not stop the tears running down my face. I felt embarrassed, but I just stood there and cried.

I tried to listen to the evidence from the pathologist Dr David Slater, and it was horrific. It was tailored strongly to fit in with the verdict that they were trying to make stick for all the victims, that every one of them had died very quickly of traumatic asphyxia and could not have been saved.

Slater described how Kevin's body was blue and bloated, which are classic symptoms apparently, and that his was the most severe case of traumatic asphyxia that he had dealt with.

He told the court Kevin's neck injury was so bad that he couldn't have spoken the word "Mum." They didn't invite the police lady to give her evidence in court because they "didn't want to run her down."

It just did not add up with what I had seen with my own eyes. When we identified Kevin's body in the Medico-Legal Centre on Watery Street in Sheffield on the Sunday, there was barely a mark on him, just a small scratch over his right eyebrow and a black fingernail on his hand.

I left the court room to go to the toilet and scream my

head off. I had tried to keep myself composed, but I just could not believe what I was hearing. In all the counselling I'd had for the past 14 months, they had been telling me he had died quickly and wouldn't have felt a thing. Now, although they were denying it in court, they were basically saying he had suffered after all.

It was so confusing. I didn't know what to think.

The social worker came looking for me and helped calm me down. I was taken into a room where Steve was and given a cup of tea. I asked Sgt Killoch, "What time did my son die?" He said he did not know.

I put the tea down and told Steve to take me home. I cried all the way back. I could not take in what they were telling me. It felt like the same journey 13 months earlier after identifying Kevin.

I spent most of the next day in the garden, crying while I was weeding and trying to get my head around what had happened. I felt like I was back to square one and Kevin had only just gone. Just as Sara was getting home from school around four o'clock, the phone went.

It was Inspector Matt Sawers from West Midlands Police asking if he could come around to talk to us about Kevin. He arrived in a big black car and carrying a briefcase. He sat himself down, sorted through his papers and proceeded to tell us he had spent most of the day with PC Derek Bruder, the off duty police officer from Merseyside who was the man trying to resuscitate Kevin in the photograph I'd been shown the day before.

PC Bruder had also not been called to give evidence, but in his statement which had been read out in court he said he had seen Kevin convulsing from his position in the stands, which is why came onto the pitch to help.

Inspector Sawers told us that Bruder had now changed his mind and thought it was more of a twitch than a convulsion. We looked at him as if he was crackers. Why had he come all this way to tell us that?

He asked if there was anything else we wanted to know. My mind was still filled with this revelation about Debra Martin, the policewoman who said Kevin had opened his eyes and called for me just before he died.

Sawers said he had been to see her as well and she was still sticking to her story, but he was very keen to emphasise Dr Slater's verdict that it just could not have happened, adding dismissively that she had not been in the police force very long, she was "off her head" and it was definitely body wind that she had heard.

As he was leaving, he just happened to mention that there was going to be another inquest on Kevin the following day, but it was only going to be concerning medical evidence and there was no need for us to go.

There was no way either of us could have faced going all that way again, so we didn't.

There was a small mention in the Liverpool Echo the next day about how Kevin's injuries had been among the worst of all the 96, but no mention at all of the two people I now knew had tried to help him.

After the mini inquests the DPP decided there was not enough evidence to prosecute and we were informed that the main inquest was to start in September 1990.

Steve was ill in bed and told me to contact our solicitor Mr Farley to find out what we should do. He said there was no need for us to get involved and the families wanted a verdict of manslaughter, but they were not going to get it.

We already knew we would have to find £3,000 if we wanted to be represented by a barrister at the inquest so we took his advice. We were ill and did not understand what was going on.

I followed what happened at the inquest as best I could through the news and the papers. It went on for 90 days, the longest in British history, and the solicitor was right. The families did not get what they wanted. The official verdict handed down was accidental death.

I was as upset and as disgusted as everybody else. Lord Justice Taylor, in his official inquiry the previous year, had put the blame squarely at the feet of South Yorkshire Police for their loss of control. Now it was nobody's fault?

What troubled me most of all, though, was the 3.15pm cut-off point that kept cropping up in all the reports.

This was the time by which, so the coroner Stefan

Popper said, that Kevin and the other victims had already received the traumatic asphyxia from which they would die and as it was such a swift cause of death, usually between four and six minutes, there was no need to hear any evidence from after that time.

Yet I had been told that Kevin had not died until 4pm. Why were they so keen to play that down? Why had they said all these horrible things about his injuries, that he was one of the worst injured, and was blue, bloated and covered in petechial haemorrhages?

I kept thinking, 'You didn't look like that, Kevin. You looked lovely when I said goodbye to you'.

In the early days I found it difficult to remember him without a photograph and I started to think maybe my mind was playing tricks and trying to protect me, as that was how I wanted to remember him.

I thought inquests were supposed to provide answers, but I was wrong.

All this one had done was raise many more questions.

5

Long Road

'I could see she was like my mum.
She just wasn't going to go away'

IF it's true that every cloud has a silver lining, then it seemed to take a long while for them to appear around the side of those dark black Hillsborough ones.

But Mum was always the first to say that what helped keep her going was the support of the many, many people who cared about what happened to the 96.

And it was thanks to two of them in particular that her long journey in search of truth and justice was set in motion.

One of them was Sheila Coleman, a researcher at Edge Hill University College in Ormskirk who had been monitoring the legal cases following the disaster. Sheila had co-written an extensive report on Hillsborough for Liverpool City Council and had attended the mini-inquest for Kevin that Mum had missed.

Mum didn't know Sheila, but had joined the Hillsborough Family Support Group to keep up to date with everything that was going on. It was only after the coroner handed down that ridiculous accidental death verdict at the main inquest in March 1991, though, that she decided to attend her first HFSG meeting.

As she tried to get her head around what she had heard in Sheffield, she began to wonder if other families were going through the same thing. Had they been given new, shock information like she had?

Had their loved ones been marked down as dead by 3.15pm when they were still alive at 4pm? Did they share concerns that the blame had been shifted from the police in the Taylor Report to seemingly no-one?

So she went to a Hillsborough Family Support Group meeting in Liverpool and was told to give Sheila a ring, which she did, the very next night.

She introduced herself to Sheila and told her that she'd lost her son, Kevin.

"Yes, I know," Sheila replied.

I think Mum was a bit taken aback at first that anyone would know about Kevin.

Sheila recalls it well: "Anne had been at a Hillsborough Family Support Group meeting, looking a bit lost. John Glover, who had lost his son Ian in the disaster, said to her, in John's way, 'You alright, girl? Did you lose someone at Hillsborough?'

"She told him about Kevin, how she was very confused over what she'd been told when she attended his mini-inquest and how subsequently it had played on her mind.

"John said 'I know someone who can help you,' and gave her my number.

"It does feel very poignant now when I think how John and Anne, two people who were at the forefront of the fight for justice for so long, should pass away within a month of one another.

"Anne and I arranged to meet to discuss Kevin's case."

Mum and Sheila took to each other straight away. They had quite a rapport and I remember Mum saying that Sheila could even out-talk her, which took some doing! Sheila wasn't the only one who played a significant part in setting Mum off on her fight for justice for Kevin, though.

Ann Adlington, a solicitor, was working for Liverpool City Council as the Hillsborough Disaster Working Party's liaison officer. It was set up by the former Leader of Liverpool City Council, Keva Coombes, to provide support and advice for families in the aftermath of the disaster.

By this point, 1991, Mum had read the transcripts

of Kevin's inquests and was aghast to find numerous things that simply didn't add up, not least the fact that he was the only one of the 96 to have had two mini-inquests.

She went to see Ann in the City Council offices and her concerns that all was not right with the way that Kev had been treated became all the more real.

"Anne first came me to see me in 1991," Ann explains, "but it must be remembered that the South Yorkshire Police had placed an embargo on the release of any witness statements to bereaved families until the conclusion of disciplinary action.

"This embargo was only lifted to a limited extent on January 13, 1992 – almost two years after the mini-inquests had concluded. Therefore, families at the mini-inquests and main inquest had no actual statements relating to the death of their loved ones.

"They simply had to rely upon a summary of those statements which had been prepared by West Midlands Police.

"The more I learned about Anne's case, the more horrified I became at how her and Steve had been treated when they went to Sheffield for that first hearing.

"The coroner's attitude to them was evident in the wildly inappropriate comment he made to Steve right at the beginning when he inferred that he was not Kevin's 'true dad' because he was his step-father. Steve later told me that it made him feel as if he had no right to be there.

"Kevin's was one of those cases where every time you read through the transcript, something else would jump out at you as being inconsistent or suspicious. Another thing that stood out was the identity of the final medical expert wheeled out at the second of Kevin's mini-inquests to tell the jury that he would have been brain-dead before he was carried out of the Leppings Lane terrace.

"He was the very same Dr Ernest Gumpert who gave identical evidence later that same year in a case to determine pre-death suffering which the families involved lost.

"A pattern was emerging."

Kirklands wine bar on Hardman Street was a bit of a party venue in the 1990s. It was a popular weekend spot for local clubbers and students. I bet some even met their partners or future husbands and wives in there.

But Kirklands was also the scene of a meeting of a very different kind. It was there that Mum and Sheila met for the first time. She once described Sheila as "my greatest ally in my search for justice," not least because in that meeting she explained to Mum what the significance of the 3.15pm cut-off point was in a way she could understand.

Mum quickly realised that the coroner's job was to inquire how, where and when a person had died, not apportion blame, but by limiting evidence to before 3.15pm he wasn't doing that because there was evidence that Kevin was still alive at 4pm.

One of the big ironies of Kevin's case was that two of the key witnesses were actually police officers.

Derek Bruder, the off-duty Merseyside bobby who was a trained first-aider, had supposedly suddenly realised that he was wrong in between the first and second inquests, and hadn't after all found a pulse on Kevin.

They hadn't even seen fit to tell Mum about that pulse when she attended the first hearing. She only found out about it when the transcripts were finally released to her in September 1991.

When it came to Debra Martin, the special police constable and trained dental nurse in whose arms Kevin died, they just described her as mad. 'Poor WPC Martin'.

Sheila continues: "It was that age-old thing of pathologizing the woman and it spoke volumes when the coroner said that.

"You smelt a rat when they went to the lengths they did to paint Bruder and Martin as unreliable witnesses while bringing in their own 'experts' to ensure everything fitted in with the picture they were trying to paint of an unruly, ungovernable mob, with the alcohol readings for every victim, including a ten-year-old boy, being read out in court.

"At the heart of the appalling way the inquest was conducted was the imposition of the 3.15pm cut-off time by the coroner.

"Even from the outset, there was talk of having it judicially reviewed at the High Court, but families were advised to wait until the verdict, by which time it was too late.

"This completely arbitrary juncture, chosen because that was the time the first ambulance arrived on the pitch, meant the inquest was quite simply an incomplete investigation.

"By preventing the jury from hearing any evidence from beyond that point, any examination of the actions of police or emergency services was prevented and this allowed the official line that none of the victims could possibly have been saved to take root."

It turned out that Mum wasn't the only one who was concerned about the inquest verdict.

A group containing another five families were also troubled by what they had heard. They felt their loved ones might still be alive if they had only received appropriate medical care so Sheila got a barrister to come to Liverpool and speak to them over what they could do about it.

"Terry Munyard, who ironically was from the same chambers as Pete Weatherby who went on to work closely with Anne in later years, gave very good advice at that meeting as to what families could do with regard to a judicial review of the inquest verdict, but was honest enough to say he wasn't prepared to take the case on himself," says Sheila.

"Eventually, we managed to get hold of a barrister who would help us, Edward Fitzgerald, who Anne and I had such high regard for.

"He said at first that he wouldn't take the cases on, but we now had a hardcore of six families who wanted to carry things forward so I asked if we could just come and see him.

"I devised a little plan where I would give a synopsis of each particular case and then say to the mum or dad of that victim, 'Is there anything you'd like to add?'

"They had, of course, been primed to tell Ed how they felt and why it was important to them. And by the end he was sufficiently moved, but also absolutely aware of the strength of the evidence. 'Ok,' he said, 'we'll give it a go.' And at that point you just knew he was one of the good guys."

Mum and the other families had no money and no entitlement to legal aid, but prepared things as best they could. Ed agreed to provide his services for free, which said everything about him.

Ann Adlington was working in the legal department in the council and between her, Mum and Sheila they compiled the evidence and found Dr Iain West, an eminent forensic pathologist, who like Ed Fitzgerald became an invaluable ally and someone Mum became very fond of.

I know that she was extremely grateful to everyone she came into contact with who gave up their time or worked for free to help her fight for truth and justice. Without such help she'd have struggled to get anywhere.

It made such a difference to know there were people out there who believed in what she thought and were prepared to do what they could professionally to support her and the other families.

Sheila continues: "I've had to time to analyse it over the years and I think it comes down to the fact that Iain West and Ed Fitzgerald, both of them part of the Establishment that we were actually battling with, were just good people who saw that there was tremendous injustice here and that their professions were being brought into disrepute by the fundamental wrongs that had been allowed to take place.

"They could quite easily have not wanted anything to do with it. Iain West in particular was outraged by how appallingly the medical work had been carried out.

"He wasn't some kind of radical pathologist, he was the man they brought in to work on IRA bombings and he did Robert Maxwell's autopsy. Ed became Sir Edward Fitzgerald. These people lived in a different world to us, but when you approached them with the truth it cut through all hierarchies."

Sheila has told me that one of the biggest things that helped at this stage was Mum's determination and perseverance. She was able to provide them with first-hand evidence to back up her beliefs about how Kevin had been treated.

She had written to South Yorkshire Police asking to see Debra Martin and Derek Bruder's initial statements, but they were refusing at that stage to release any information to do with Hillsborough because there were still outstanding disciplinary proceedings against the two policemen nominally in charge on the day, David Duckenfield and Bernard Murray.

However, Mum managed to take their intransigence out of the equation, in the case of Derek Bruder at least, by displaying a tremendous piece of initiative.

Mum had a brainwave. She was sick of hearing excuse after excuse from South Yorkshire Police when she suddenly realised that she didn't need to get through them to speak to Derek Bruder. She was at home listening to 'Home by the Sea' when she made the snap decision to phone the Merseyside Police headquarters at Canning Place.

She simply asked to speak to "Mr Bruder, PC 7808," having seen his number on the inquest papers, and discovered he was based at Hope Street police station.

He wasn't there, but within a couple of hours she had a meeting arranged with him at the station in 48 hours time on the Sunday.

She asked Sheila to attend with her and they soon discovered the lengths that the authorities were prepared to go to in order to make their version of events the accepted truth.

I know that Derek has admitted he felt daunted at the prospect of meeting Mum. In fact he only decided to do so after chatting to his own mum about the situation.

They talked it out and he felt that if his mother was ever in Anne's position with regard to himself then he would want somebody to step forward.

So Derek was perfectly willing to meet with Mum, but Merseyside Police seemed reluctant to let it happen at first. They insisted that his inspector, Peter Edge, should be in attendance.

"Anne asked me a number of questions which I answered honestly and transparently as best I could," remembers Derek. "It was quite upsetting for her and also for me. I did struggle to keep my emotions in check, but just about managed because it was very important to me that she got an honest and truthful account of the last minutes of her son's life.

"I was shell-shocked by the way my evidence was not presented in its entirety or in a professional manner at the two inquests. It did not represent what happened on the day.

"I know that from my position in the stand I saw Kevin moving or convulsing on the ground where he lay, that I found a pulse when I came onto the pitch to try to resuscitate him and that during this time I tried to flag down an ambulance that came onto the pitch at 3.37pm, all pieces of information that I confirmed in the official statement I made twelve days after the disaster.

"But, having completely neglected to even mention the pulse first time around, the second inquest hearing two days later was told that I had changed my version of events to say I 'may have been mistaken' about finding it and also that I now thought the convulsion I had seen was more of a twitch."

Quite understandably, one of the first questions Mum asked him was "why did you change your statement?"

He told her how a West Midlands Detective Inspector, Matthew Sawers, came to his house on May 3, 1990, the day in between Kevin's two inquests, and spoke with him for about six hours.

It was apparent to Derek after the first 20 minutes what Sawers was trying to do.

"He had knocked on my door with the agenda of trying to change my mind about a number of points to do with the young man I had tried to help at Hillsborough," Derek states. "It was only on that day that I learned that individual had been Kevin Williams. I had asked for his name at the time of my original statement, but they wouldn't tell me.

"Sawers attempted to persuade me that I was wrong

about various medical issues to do with Kevin, but after about four hours it was clear that we were getting nowhere.

"He asked if he could use my telephone and then handed me the receiver to talk to Dr Slater, the pathologist who had carried out Kevin's autopsy.

"He tried to change my view that I found a pulse on Kevin, questioning whether I had taken it properly and also whether the convulsion I had seen from the stand had in fact been a twitch.

"I remember him using medical terms to explain how sometimes there is a build up of gases inside a dead body which can cause it to wriggle slightly and I could have mistaken this for the movement that I had witnessed.

"I said to him, 'If what you're putting to me is that it is medically possible that I took the pulse incorrectly then how I am in any position to argue. I'm not a doctor, you are. If you're telling me that in the throes of death, a number of things can happen, then I have to accept that possibility on the basis of your medical knowledge. However I know what I believe, I know how to take a pulse and that boy had a pulse.'

"My conversation with Slater was fairly brief, but Sawers then went on to explain how all the video recordings and TV footage of the tragedy had been studied by the inquiry team and the ambulance mentioned by me as entering the stadium at 3.37pm in my first statement could not have been correct as there was no evidence to support this.

"He went on to say that it could have been my imagination playing tricks as there were many things going on at the time and that I could have been mistaken.

"This really annoyed me and I told him that I was not mistaken, nor did I imagine the ambulance. I insisted that he made reference to it in the further statement he took."

Mum believed their objective was quite clear – to show the jury that if he was wrong about the ambulance, his other evidence could then be discredited as well.

In light of the differences between his beliefs as to what happened and the medical opinion, Derek fully expected to be called to the inquest in order to clarify the obvious grey areas which had emerged.

He was very surprised not to be and horrified at how his testimony was presented the following day, and at the main inquest the following year.

It painted him as an unreliable witness and basically called into question his honesty and his competence.

"It's ironic," added Derek, "you try and keep your integrity intact because you go to a football match and witness carnage so you step up and do your best. To have it absolutely destroyed like that was a kick in the guts because I was only there trying to help someone.

"For that to then happen tore my heart out. It made

me wonder what it was all really about. There were obviously bigger issues at play rather than just me trying to save a young boy who was struggling and consequently died.

"It was gut-wrenching, although after that first meeting with Anne I always had a feeling that this wasn't the end. I could see there was a real tenacity about her.

"My mum is the same. She is similarly meek and mild woman, but if it was her children she would absolutely make it her life's mission to find the truth.

"Within five minutes of meeting Anne Williams I could see my own mum.

"I just knew she wasn't going to go away."

Derek was not prepared to make another statement although he did say he would give evidence should there be another inquest. In January 1992, only a few weeks after Mum's meeting with him, a further opportunity for progress presented itself.

David Duckenfield had retired in November 1991 due to ill-health, thus avoiding the disciplinary action for neglect of duty hanging over him. On January 13, 1992, the Police Complaints Authority (now the IPCC) decided that it would be unfair to proceed against Bernard Murray alone. Mum and the other five immediately wrote asking for the Martin and Bruder statements again.

It already looked like Debra Martin's evidence would

be crucial at this stage, but they didn't know if she still worked for the police.

They wrote to Brian Mole, who was by now in charge of police information in his role as Chief Superintendent, Complaints and Discipline. He had been match commander at the 1988 semi-final and had originally been appointed to that position for the 1989 semi-final, which shows how incestuous the South Yorkshire force had all become. They demonstrated a need to maintain control over the release of information at any cost.

They were guarding information as closely as possible. Mole told the group that he'd written to the witnesses for permission to release the statements. Mum also got our local MP involved, Sir Malcolm Thornton, who wrote to the Attorney General Sir Patrick Mayhew.

He did not feel there was sufficient grounds for a new inquest, but did say he would try to ensure that the coroner released those statements.

In the meantime, Mum and the other five families took a flyer and wrote a letter to Debra Martin, care of the South Yorkshire Police personnel department, and asked for it to be forwarded onto her as they didn't have her address.

They did, and the next thing they knew she had got in touch with Mum and agreed to come to Formby to meet her in February 1992.

Ann Adlington takes up the story. "Anne asked myself and Sheila Coleman to attend and we sat in Anne's living room for hours while Debra told us in graphic and painful detail her experiences at Hillsborough and afterwards.

"Her fear that she had passed out briefly in the chaos outside the ground. Her desperation to save Kevin as she tried to resuscitate him. Her despair as he opened his eyes and called for Anne before dying in her arms. Her disgust as other police officers stuffed their faces with fried chicken as they waited for hours with the bodies in the gymnasium-turned-mortuary. And the deep emotional impact the experience had had upon her at the time, and ever since.

"Like Bruder, she had been visited in her home by an investigating West Midlands officer, Sergeant Julie Appleton, and pressurised into making a second statement which differed significantly from her first one and which fitted more in line with the version of events which the authorities were desperate to make stick.

"A particularly notable omission from her second statement was the part where Kevin had opened his eyes and spoken before passing away.

"Having been pursued at work and at home over a number of weeks by the West Midlands force, she felt so harassed she admitted to having not even read the second statement before signing.

"I was very careful not to lead her in any way, but every so often she would refer back to her dealings with

Kevin and she was absolutely consistent about how she helped Kevin and the final moments of his life.

"I took a third statement from her at our meeting. This backed up the events described in her first statement and at least set the record straight from her point of view."

On a personal level, Mum was hugely grateful to Debra for how she had looked after Kevin. She had wiped his face, combed his hair and made him presentable after he had died. More than that, she had cared for him and, Mum felt, given him some comfort in his last moments. That meant an awful lot to her.

However, Debra's account of events led to even more questions. Mum continued working towards the judicial review along with the other five families who were involved. The evidence obtained by Mum gave her an advantage over other families who were still trying to obtain witness statements.

Therefore, Mum's case was given more prominence for that single, very good reason. It was by far the strongest case and had the potential to open the door for everybody else.

A memorial, the legal name for a submission of evidence, to the Attorney General asking for a new inquest under Section 13 of the Coroners Act was rejected. However, Edward Fitzgerald still felt they had scope to go for a judicial review of the original accidental death verdict, particularly in view of the imposition of the 3.15pm cut-off time. They had to apply for leave, or permission, from a judge at the High Court first. With the full support of Ann and the Council's Working Party, Mum and the others all travelled to London to try and secure it.

The other five families were John and Theresa Glover, Sandra and Jimmy Stringer, Joan and Peter Tootle, Doreen and Les Jones, and Joan Sinclair.

"When we got the green light to proceed, on April 6, 1993," says Ann Adlington, "it was the first victory that any of the families had ever had in relation to Hillsborough. We were ecstatic when it was granted and we went to the pub over the road from the court, The George, in a state of blissful shock.

"Ed Fitzgerald came with us and bought us a celebratory drink when we felt that it was us who should be thanking him.

"When that leave to proceed was granted, some of the six families qualified for legal aid which enabled them to instruct Alun Jones QC, who had worked with Ed on controversial inquests previously, so that added to the experience of our team.

"He was also fearless in Court, refusing to be brow beaten by the judiciary.

"He would stand, fists clenched, arguing his case fiercely. On several occasions, the judges would condescendingly put him down, forcing him to sit down and pause for reflection. Then he would return to his feet and frame his argument in a different manner.

"I felt that the judicial review had a good chance of succeeding because the 3.15pm cut-off point imposed by the coroner made neither rhyme nor reason.

"It was a deeply flawed concept which I always thought had been put in place to limit any potential compensation payouts. This can be evidenced by the presence of South Yorkshire Police insurance solicitor Peter Metcalfe at the pre-inquest hearings, the parameters being set in place quite early.

"Other families as well as Anne had managed to secure pieces of evidence and we knew at least four of the six victims in question were alive after 3.15pm.

"Therefore, very strong representations were made to the High Court. Undoubtedly, those representations demonstrated that there had been insufficiency of enquiry at the inquests and that evidence had been suppressed. These were both grounds upon which a new inquest could be ordered.

"The case came up for hearing in London in the first week of November 1993, at the same time as the trial of James Bulger's killers was taking place in Preston. This was probably no coincidence.

"The City's name had taken a battering in the national and international media. The families' case attracted almost no media coverage and it soon became clear that we had little hope of success.

"The judges had been changed quite late and our lawyers felt that this would not help our case. The ambulance authority would not even recognise the existence of the ambulance that was crucial in proving the veracity of Derek Bruder's evidence and one of the judges in his judgment couldn't even get the names of the teams involved in the match that day correct, referring to a semi-final between Liverpool and Sheffield Wednesday.

"Although not a surprise, it was a terrible feeling when the verdict came back: 'not in the interests of justice' for a fresh inquest to be held."

Mum felt this became even more galling when the Hillsborough Independent Panel released their documents almost 20 years later, revealing correspondence from within the Attorney General's office that acknowledged Kevin's case was different.

There was just no way she was going to be allowed to win at that point. They had made things difficult for her every step of the way.

Ed Fitzgerald had been surprised that the group were granted leave to even go for it. Mum and the other families had been nervously awaiting the release of post-mortem photos due to be released by South Yorkshire Police to Iain West to enable him to draft his expert medical report. The last of these was released on the Friday before the hearing was due to start.

In the course of the judicial review, Alun Jones was given an index of statements said to be held by the South Yorkshire Police. This index was disclosed only because there was some doubt as to whether a second statement of a witness relevant to one the cases had been provided. This index ran to 116 pages, and it listed 3,907 statements.

So it was quite clear that thousands of witness statements had been made in relation to Hillsborough, but Mum only got to see perhaps two dozen of them at the most.

A whole body of evidence existed that nobody was allowed to scrutinise at that time, nor would relevant statements be released for at least another five years.

After the judicial review, Mum was advised that legally there was now nowhere left to go. That might have been in for a less determined woman. Not Mum!

Having seen what a mess the authorities had made of their investigations, she had already begun conducting her own one and was not going to stop until she got the justice that she and all the other families deserved.

6

A New Approach

'Everyone was so flat travelling home.
It was a really dark time for her'

MANY people have asked how Mum kept going for so long with all the knock-backs.

It's quite simple. She knew she was right. She knew Kevin should still be with us and from the minute she found out that he had called for her, that was it. She was a woman on a mission.

People would comment on how far she'd gone for Kev and say things like he must have been her favourite, but she would have done the same for any of us. It almost seemed like the more doors got slammed in her face, the more determined she became to keep going.

That's not to say that she didn't have times when she was fed up with it all, her "downers," as she used to call them.

There were plenty of times when she felt like giving up. She just didn't. And it helped that she was gradually building a network of people around her who would help keep her going when she needed a lift.

Sheila, as ever, was one of those people. The two of them would always be getting together and brainstorming who might be able to help move the campaign forward. They would get hunches and follow them up. 'Maybe so and so might help us...' and so on. No-one was off the radar. If they thought they might be able to help, they would approach them. They saw no barriers to doing that.

Of course, nothing was straightforward. Often they would get passed from person to person. When you don't know where to start getting hold of someone important then you can easily get lost in the system.

It was at one of those meetings, probably in a cafe, that Sheila and Mum stumbled upon a man who could help them understand just how easily Kevin could have been saved. A man who put them in a stronger position to challenge the 'facts'.

That man was Dr James Burns, a Home Office pathologist in Liverpool. The meeting took place in the Royal Liverpool Hospital. After making them coffee, he used models to explain the complicated medical points in more detail. He was quite clear about one fact: There was no way that the official number of post-mortems could have been carried out properly in the time allocated.

It was another small step on the road. Another little piece of evidence that pointed them in the right direction.

"You know where I am if you need me," he said as Sheila and Mum were leaving. He refused to take any payment for his time. Again, it was comforting for Mum to know she could rely on these professionals and call upon them again if needs be.

Mum got to know people of this calibre by basically knocking on their doors and saying "Look, this has happened and it stinks, can you help us?" Professional people holding the top jobs in the city. Influential men and women who knew their area of expertise inside out. I know Mum, Shelia, Ann and other families had a lot of doors shut in their faces, but many good people opened them for them too.

Over time, from travelling here there and everywhere together, Mum became firm friends with Sheila. Hillsborough became part of their lives so they had lots of shared experiences, but also much in common beyond that – kids, families and so on.

Sheila says: "I got to know a lot about Anne and her life, and how she grew up.

"She wasn't from Liverpool and that was quite obvious to a Scouser! She was quite different to someone who'd grown up in an inner city, where you have to wise up quite quickly. She was distinct from many of the other families that I worked with in the sense that she wasn't from Liverpool, although very much of Liverpool in the end.

"She was still traumatised from the loss of Kevin and painfully shy when I first met her. She didn't really make eye contact and would hide behind her hair. She used to try and cover her birthmark with it but she didn't in the end, which was great. You can trace her emerging confidence through photographs.

"Initially, though, she was very in on herself because of the grief.

"We used to meet for a bite to eat in Kirklands quite regularly. I was lecturing in sociology at Hope University and she would meet me at lunch time but say 'Oh I don't want anything to eat.' Her whole nervous system was in turmoil.

"I'd say, 'Just get a sandwich' and what I noticed early on was that, because I was able to make her laugh a bit, as she started to relax, she'd start nibbling on the food a little without even realising.

"I got into the habit of consciously trying to make her laugh in order to get her to eat."

It wasn't all work, work, work. The intensity of the campaign made it a necessity to have a break from time to time. It's true that because of Mum's background, there were parts of Liverpool she had never seen. Her friendship with Sheila changed that. Up until now, Sefton Park and Lark Lane were places Mum had never been to.

I don't know how it came up, but it turned out that Sheila took an afternoon off once to show her around the south of the city. It was a bit of breathing space. A welcome few hours of leisure time away from the complexities and demands of the fight for justice.

Sheila cared about Mum and knew that it was important for her to have a break from it. She helped her reach a point where she could think, 'I'm putting Hillsborough to one side for a bit' and actually give herself a rest from it all for a while.

The friendship led to different things, the kind of things friends do for each other. Mum even minded Sheila's dog Frither when she went on holiday to Greece. Her cats had been put in a cattery, but it was so expensive that Mum said she would happily look after the dog along with her own cats.

Sheila had found Frither when she was a little puppy in a market. She was a lovely, faithful old dog. Mum met Sheila in town and Frither trotted off to Formby with her quite happily.

"I went away on holiday," Sheila recalls, "but I was still worrying, thinking 'I hope Frither will be alright' because even though I had cats myself and Frither was used to them, she was getting on a bit. She was 19 when she died. Anyway, when I came back from holiday, Frither didn't want to come home! The weather had been beautiful while I was away and she spent most of the time lying on a sun lounger next to Anne in the garden. Anne would always ask after Frither afterwards."

The two friends made good progress and got everything together for the judicial review, but it was obvious from quite early on that they wouldn't win.

It was difficult at the time for them to see the bigger picture, that they were always going to lose. The political climate saw to that and it was easy for Mum and Sheila, as she admitted, to be cynical of the way things were at that level of the Establishment.

"There was a part of me that felt 'here's the evidence, we're telling the truth, we're in the right, you've got to listen to us'," Sheila says. "But they didn't."

So, despite expecting the worst, it was awful when they did lose. To be hit with the reality. To realise that you can tell the truth and they can still cover it up.

That was when I knew Mum had taken it badly.

It was a long train journey home from London on that Bonfire Night in 1993. Autumn had long taken hold and the nights were getting longer. The train seemed to take forever. Everyone was so flat travelling home to Liverpool. It was awful. A really dark time for her.

When she got home, I could see that Mum was really down. She was so down that, for a split second, she wanted to put a stop to all the campaigning. It was then that she decided to do something really serious – she said she was going to burn all the Hillsborough papers in the garden.

I had to stop her. I had to do something about it. I couldn't let all the hard work that had gone in turn to ashes. The thought of all the carefully collected paperwork going up in flames was too much to take.

I had a big cabin bed at the time. It was the kind of bed that had doors on where the kids could put their books and toys. I took the doors off and hid all the Hillsborough papers inside. They were safe in there. Mum would never guess where they were.

Of course, it was all an empty threat. A black moment. A moment that passed. She calmed down a bit and we all moved on.

I could understand her reaction. Everyone felt that there was nowhere to go. There wasn't really. But while Mum would say that, while she may have threatened to burn the papers, deep down I know she refused to accept it.

She was an ordinary person who had lost the son she loved. Nobody could change that fact. She would always be Kevin's Mum and driven to do what was right for him.

Sheila knew that Mum was damaged through the experience of fighting for justice. She thought, at times, she appeared incredibly fragile, so much so that she seemed on the point of collapse. Despite all that, it showed that Mum had an inner-strength that she may never have discovered if not for what she went through with Hillsborough.

"I don't think she believed in herself much in the early years," says Sheila. "From what she told me about her upbringing, she was largely invisible as a kid. She used to speak very positively about her grandfather and her brothers, Danny and Chris, but I realised that she hadn't had a very easy life, even before Hillsborough.

"No-one had ever really nurtured confidence in her and her first marriage was very traumatic for her as well, but over time she derived this inner fortitude that was incredible."

Mum was always willing to learn. If learning was what was required to progress, she would do it. Anything to help the cause. She went on a course to learn computer skills and developed a very organised filing system with her campaign because it was so important to her.

Sheila managed to get hold of five video tapes of the BBC coverage from the day and Mum spent hours going through them to try and find anything that could help Kevin's case, managing to pinpoint the moments when he was lifted from the pens by PC Michael Craighill and was being tended to on the pitch.

It was that drive that made her look for a different approach after the disappointment of the Judicial Review.

Mum was right in her view that the media coverage

had been inadequate, almost to the point of being non-existent, so she wrote an 18-page letter to all the main television documentary programmes because she felt not enough people knew about the injustice of Hillsborough.

David Alford, a researcher from the Cook Report got in touch, to say that Roger Cook was interested in what Mum had to say. There were mixed views over him and his doorstepping approach, but he is an excellent journalist.

Mum and Sheila were suspicious beforehand, though, inevitably after the way the media in general had dealt with Hillsborough up to that point. Would he do what he said he was going to do or would it just be a hatchet job?

Alford came to see her and apparently he went back to Roger Cook and told him he was mightily impressed with what Mum had told him. He realised that Mum obviously knew what she was talking about, had done an enormous amount of digging and had some powerful substance to what she was saying. She'd impressed him.

Roger Cook himself then travelled to Formby to meet Mum and came away convinced that the mainstream media's towing of the official line was completely wrong. That the victims were not the authors of their own misfortune. That they were not all dead by 3.15pm.

They went ahead and made a programme on that basis. Cook discovered fairly early on that the Hillsborough ground did not have the required safety certificate and managed to trace the only paramedic, Tony Edwards, who had been allowed to make it onto the pitch.

His evidence was shocking in itself because it went completely against what had been presented to the Taylor Inquiry and the inquests. They had been told that ambulances were unable to get into the stadium because of unsuitable ramps, but Tony told them that simply was not true. Like Derek Bruder, he had offered to give evidence in person, but not been called.

He informed them that there had been a police cordon at the Penistone Lane end which would not let any of the 44 ambulances in attendance through because they said the fans were "still fighting in there."

Having learned over his radio that there were fatalities in the ground, Tony managed to get into Hillsborough by putting on his two-tone lights and mowing through the cordon, but none of the other ambulances followed him.

Poor Tony was then in the terrible position of having to choose who, out of the hundreds of people needing help, to take to hospital.

Finding him was important in enabling Mum to show how the police impeded the emergency response, such as it was, but it was also absolutely vital in validating

Derek Bruder's evidence, which put her in a strong position when Cook managed to persuade the coroner Stefan Popper to be interviewed.

Popper would not be shaken from his insistence that everyone was dead, or as good as, by 3.15pm, even though there was evidence from one of the country's leading consultant forensic pathologists, Dr Iain West, who confirmed there was no way Kevin was dead at that time. That the injuries he suffered were not traumatic asphyxia and had he been attended to properly he might have survived, which as we now know, was the case for as many as 58 others.

Popper's conviction was shaken, however, when Cook pushed him over PC Bruder and what he still, at that stage, maintained was a phantom ambulance.

Cook said: "'If Mr Bruder was in error on the ambulance he might have been in error over the other things,'" Popper told me. When I informed him that Bruder was correct because we had now found the ambulance, he could only reply, "'Oh, but at the time we didn't know it.'"

"We also 'bounced' David Duckenfield, who had a reputation for never taking responsibility for anything and had the nickname 'Duck-and-weave'.

"We door-stepped him at his golf club. He was furious and wouldn't answer any questions. We later got a letter saying 'This man is ill, he retired on medical grounds due to post-traumatic stress'. I ask you…"

They had all this evidence and were miles ahead of everyone else, but couldn't get any of the Establishment, or even MPs, to take it seriously. That made Cook very cross.

Roger stayed in touch with Mum over the years because, in his words, "she was a very impressive woman."

"Even when she was turned down in Europe, which would have killed many people stone dead, she said it just made her want to carry on even more," continued Cook. "But it did, of course, cost her dearly, first of all in terms of her marriage and then her health.

"She was able to keep going for so long in the face of all the knock-backs because she knew she was right. She was a very principled woman. She had to put up with a lot of politics.

"Some of the people you might have expected to be on her side had a downer on her because they thought she was only concerned about Kevin.

"She ended up having to plough a lonely furrow at times, but she always maintained the strength of the evidence in Kevin's case could be key in unlocking the story for everyone else and that proved to be true.

"It was only from the outside she had this steely determination. She was a very warm woman and had a lovely nature.

"Whenever we would have email conversations or telephone calls, because I wanted her to update me on what was happening, you almost had to force the information out of her because she'd be too busy asking me how I was and what I was up to.

"She was a very special lady."

Sheila and Mum knew they had no resources because they didn't have any money. What the Cook Report enabled them to do was continue to say 'we'd like to find this person or that person' and because they had the backing and the real investigative know-how they were able to put a lot more of the jigsaw pieces in place.

I'm sure that there was a level at which they might have found it quite exciting, working with the producers and tracking people down like in a detective novel or Cagney and Lacey.

They had to break rules, sometimes. If laws are unjust, then they should be broken.

At one stage, Sheila knew that one of the groups in the Hillsborough Centre on Stanley Park had access to some video tapes that they needed so they 'borrowed' them for a couple of hours. The two of them rented a room at the Adelphi so they could set up the dual recorders to copy them from one tape to another and slipped back in to return them before they had to lock up at nine o'clock at night.

It paid off, too, because that is how they found Tony Edwards. Those tapes had been there all the time but no-one had been allowed access to them, which was crazy. Social services played a policing role at times

over Hillsborough and worked closely with the West
Midlands Police leading up to, and during, the inquests.

There was an occasion when Sheila drove with the
Cook Report team to the house in Tuebrook where she
thought George Tomkins was living. She had read an
article in the paper about the corruption he'd suffered
at the hands of West Midlands Police and he proved
to be an invaluable ally to Mum and us all in the fight
for justice.

George had been fitted up for an armed robbery he
did not commit in 1983 and spent 17 months on re-
mand in Winson Green prison before being acquitted.
He made a formal complaint that he had been set up
by Detective Superintendent Stanley Beechey and in
March 1996 eventually won a civil case against West
Midlands Police, with them agreeing to pay £40,000
compensation and £70,000 in legal costs while still refusing to admit any wrongdoing.

Beechey had been part of the force's Serious Crimes
Squad that, even by police standards of the time, was
regarded as seriously out of control. Allegations of mal-
practice, brutality and corruption were commonplace
on their watch and they had been involved in numerous miscarriages of justice, including the Birmingham
Six and Bridgewater Four.

Less than a fortnight after the interim Taylor Report
was released in August 1990, they were disbanded by
their chief constable Geoffrey Dear who announced an

investigation into their actions would be forthcoming.

Yet incredibly, even with this hanging over them, just two days later West Midlands was announced as the force who would be compiling the report on criminal investigations over Hillsborough and examining the role of their South Yorkshire counterparts.

Officers from the disgraced Serious Crimes Squad had been put on 'non-operational duties' while the investigations into their insidious actions were being carried out, but Stanley Beechey was brought in to study 'technical aspects' of Hillsborough and went on to play a significant role in the inquests.

He became right-hand man to Stefan Popper, who described him as his 'second most senior officer' and prepared summaries of witness evidence at the mini-inquests, receiving a gushing tribute from the coroner as well as taking part in the criminal investigation and the main inquest itself the following year.

This was all while Beechey himself was under investigation and was supposed to be being kept to low-level involvement in non-frontline police matters.

It was yet another example of how the integrity of the legal processes that followed Hillsborough was utterly compromised.

Aside from his own experiences at the hands of the West Midlands Police, George was a Liverpool man and was outraged at how the families and survivors had been treated. He was unable to take part in the Cook

Report because it could have jeopardised his own case, but he was happy to come on board to try and help Mum in any way he could. He was so generous with his time and his information, and went on to become a valued member of the Hillsborough Justice Campaign.

"We learned a lot from George," Sheila says, "and also became friends along the way. George, Anne and I had our little routine before going to weekly HJC meetings. I would go to the gym in the Adelphi and Anne would come up to Liverpool and meet me.

"We would have our tea in a really nice pizza place they used to have there then transfer to Kimos to meet George and all go together to meet the others at the HJC shop. We would meet Monday after Monday and for a lot of that time there was absolutely nothing going on legally."

It was a handful of people like Sheila and George who kept things going through what were the dark years. It was their encouragement that helped Mum chip away at all the obstacles and people that were in her way.

Two's company: Anne with brother Danny growing up in Formby during the 1950s

Early days: A school photo showing Anne in pigtails and on holiday in Jersey in the late 1950s

New family: Anne on her wedding day to Steve in 1978 (above, right) and (above, left) after Sara was born in 1979. Left: Anne and Danny (with beard) at brother Chris and Kim's wedding

Happy family: Anne with (left to right) Michael, Sara and Kevin in 1981

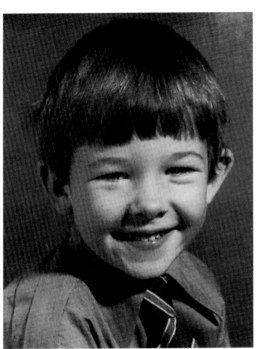

First school picture: Anne's favourite photo of Kevin, taken when he was aged just five

Memories: Michael, Sara and Kevin at Christmas, 1988 and Kevin on a school trip to Austria the same year.
Left: A school picture of Michael and Kevin

Never forget:
Anne with a picture of Kevin and (right) the memorial wall to Kevin at Formby High School

KEVIN WILLIAMS 27.5.73

KEVIN

HILLSBOROUGH
15.4.89

You'll Never Walk Alone!

HILLSBOROUGH MEMORIAL SERVICE

THE FIRST ANNIVERSARY OF HILLSBOROUGH

EASTER SUNDAY
April 15th, 1990,
2.45 p.m.
at ANFIELD

One year on: The first anniversary of Hillsborough and the first memorial service at Anfield as fans gather in 1990 to remember the victims

Centre of attention:
Kenny and Marina Dalglish at the opening of the Hillsborough Centre in 1990. Right: Kenny holds baby Thomas and (below) Peter Carney with Marina

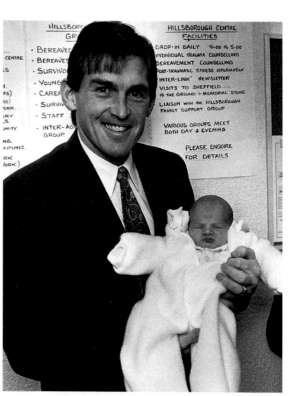

On the right track:
The families arrive back in Liverpool after having won a judicial review of the inquests in April, 1993

Pulling together:
Sara with a banner made for Kevin at school and (below) Anne presents the Kevin Williams Cup at Formby High School in the early 1990s

The dark years: Anne never lost hope even when it seemed as though the Hillsborough campaign had come to the end of the road

Always in our thoughts: A mosaic on the Kop ten years on from the disaster

7

Heroes

'Robbing the dead? How?
They were too busy trying to save them'

OF all the sickening aspects of Hillsborough, there were few things that made Mum's blood boil as much as the treatment of the survivors. The lies started barely ten minutes after the referee stopped the match at 3.06pm.

While the police were preventing the ambulances from getting into the ground and the so-called 'hooligans' were ripping down advertising hoardings to use as stretchers because the officers on the pitch were too busy forming a cordon to stop an imaginary riot, the blame was already – and quite disgracefully – being put on the shoulders of Liverpool supporters.

Unconfirmed reports that Liverpool fans had kicked a gate down and forced their way into the stadium were already being broadcast on BBC radio. In reality, many of those Liverpool supporters were still running around the Hillsborough pitch − the patch of green grass their heroes should've been playing on against Nottingham Forest for a place in the FA Cup final − trying to save lives.

No wonder those reports were unconfirmed. They weren't true.

The 'gate forced open' story came from what the policeman in charge, David Duckenfield, had told FA chief executive Graham Kelly when he'd gone up to the police control room to find out what was going on. And, while that lying bastard soon had to backtrack after CCTV footage showed he had actually given the order to open the gate himself, the damage was done.

The seed had been sown in people's minds and by the time The Sun newspaper − 'The Scum' as I call it − really went to town on the Wednesday afterwards with the police-led smear campaign that Liverpool fans were to blame, the idea had taken a firm hold. It had become a fact for many. One that even now, after everything that has since transpired, some still believe.

It didn't matter to these sheep that the Taylor Report praised the actions of the fans and put the blame squarely on the police.

They just believed what they had been told by those

looking to get themselves off the hook. For years we had to listen to all that rubbish about how the Liverpool fans killed their own and had robbed from the dead. Scouse stereotyping used to smear a city in the worst possible way. Despicable.

The lie that used to really make Mum blow her top, truly wind her up, was the 'robbing the dead' claims. "How?" she would say. "They were too busy trying to save them."

The fact is that many more people would have died but for the Liverpool fans on that horrendous day.

Even though plenty were dazed and injured themselves, they sprung into action to start the rescue operation while too many supposedly trained professionals stood around doing nothing.

The survivors were the forgotten victims of Hillsborough. They went through hell that day and it left many of them with an awful lot of mental issues to try and deal with, not least the guilt at having survived when 96 of their fellow Reds didn't.

You can see physical injuries, but not mental trauma. For some, if not all, of those surviving Liverpool supporters, the horrific memories of what they witnessed will never go away. They're like an invisible scar. One that can haunt you forever. To then be told that the disaster was their own fault. That they were responsible. That they had, in effect, killed their mates wasn't just cruel. It was inhuman.

The people that peddled those lies have blood on their hands because no-one will ever know the true cost of Hillsborough.

Ninety-six died, but there have been many more casualties. Suicides. Breakdowns. Divorces. Alcoholism. Drug problems. Mental torment.

Lives have been damaged, sometimes beyond repair, because too many didn't care about the walking wounded and about how the horror they experienced and the manufactured myths would affect their minds. About how they'd cope. About what they went through both on April 15 and in the aftermath.

Almost 25 years on − a quarter-of-a-century later − they're still going through it.

Thankfully, there were some good people who did care. Who did help. Who gave the families of the 96 and the survivors strength.

One of the first times I really noticed that people were still interested and wanted to help was when we went to Anfield on a matchday to hand out leaflets.

Mum had finally managed to persuade South Yorkshire Police to release some of the photographs they had of Kevin and in one of them it showed Derek Bruder trying to revive him on the pitch. Another lad, in a white jumper, was holding Kev's head.

She wanted to find everyone who had had anything to do with Kev on the day so we got 5,000 posters printed off through a friend of Sheila's that could do them cheaply. It was addressed to 'all Liverpool fans' and had a picture of Kevin, with the words 'This little boy died at Hillsborough. Kevin Daniel Williams, aged 15'.

Alongside it was the other picture of the mystery 'friend' helping Derek Bruder with words saying: 'This boy helped him. If anyone knows him, please contact me'. Our phone number was at the bottom.

It was August, the opening day of the 1993/94 season, and Liverpool were playing Sheffield Wednesday, which was a bit of a strange coincidence. Nigel Clough was making his debut and scored twice.

I went and stood by the Shankly Gates, near the Hillsborough memorial, while Mum covered the Kop end, which was still all-standing at the time. We had a few volunteers walking around the ground with the rest of the leaflets.

It was a baking hot day. The sun was shining brightly – just like it was on April 15, 1989 – and we dished the leaflets out in no time. A few people thought they, or a mate, might know the person we were looking for. Loads of other Liverpool supporters wished us luck. We felt hopeful we'd find the lad in the white jumper.

That night we got lots of phone calls at home – this was before anyone had mobile phones or email – but not from the lad in the photograph. Mum was disappointed, but as ever she just got on with things.

Eventually, he came forward.

He was a lad called Johnny Prescott, from Bootle, who saw himself on The Cook Report when it was aired in June 1994. It was a while after the programme when he actually got in touch with Mum, not long after he'd become a father for the first time. It can't have been an easy thing for him to do.

He didn't know Kev, but was just trying to help and agreed to give Mum a statement saying he was alive when he and Derek Bruder attended to him on the pitch. Johnny even drove her all the way home to Formby after she'd gone down to Bootle on the train see him, which was kind.

What had really opened Mum's eyes, though, was the sheer number of survivors that rang our house on the night we gave out those flyers. Most of them just wanted someone to talk to about Hillsborough.

Mum said she felt a bit like a Samaritan by the end, but it told her just how affected people still were by what had happened to them. Many felt the need to tell her that they hadn't been drunk, proof of the impact of those horrible lies.

It was thanks to another police photograph, one found by The Cook Report researchers, that two more of the survivors who helped Kevin that day, who would both go on to be very important to Mum, came into the picture.

One of them was Stevie Hart, a dad-of-four and a lifelong Liverpudlian.

Stevie first made himself known to Mum in 1994 after an appeal in the Liverpool Echo. Mum was trying to find the people who had carried Kevin on the pitch and the paper ran an appeal on the front page with a picture of Stevie and the other lads running across the pitch, carrying an advertising hoarding with Kev on.

He hadn't seen the paper initially, but he told Mum that his phone just starting ringing non-stop.

"My niece rang up and told me about the Echo," Stevie recalls. "I didn't believe her at first, but more and more people kept calling and saying 'that's you in the paper' so I walked up to the shop to get a copy. Sure enough, there I was on the front page.

"There was a phone number attached to the appeal to contact Anne, but at first I was thinking, 'do I really want to do this?'

"For the first few years I dealt with Hillsborough by just blocking it out altogether. I put it to the back of my mind and just refused to even think about it, let alone talk to anyone.

"Five years had gone by, I was doing alright with things and I had to ask myself, 'do I want to go down this road?'

"I talked it over with my wife Chris and she said. 'You've got to imagine if it was us. What would we want someone to do?'

"I thought straight away, 'you can't be more honest than that, she's absolutely right' so I called Anne up.

Right off the bat she said 'I've had all sorts of people phoning me, everyone knows you!'"

Mum arranged to meet Stevie in Liverpool at the same time she was meeting some of Roger Cook's team. She showed him a photograph of Kevin and asked if he recognised him, which he did. Immediately.

She then asked him to describe what happened on the pitch from when he was with Kev to when he left him.

Stevie knew it wasn't going to be easy revisiting that day. "It was difficult going into it after all that time, in the middle of a pub with people I didn't even know, but I had to do it because Kevin was definitely alive when I was with him. I was convinced up until the day I met Anne that he had survived.

"I had thought about him periodically and it never entered my head that he hadn't made it. I assumed that he'd been taken care of when we left him.

"Honestly... I expected Kevin to come walking out that day and for Anne to say thanks for helping us. I didn't have a clue that he was dead.

"I can't remember how many injured Liverpool fans I helped to carry on the day. Anne said she'd seen me carrying a couple of other lads from the video footage that she'd gone through. It was like a battlezone on that pitch, it was surreal.

"I had rib injuries myself that I think had been done outside of the ground when I got smashed against a wall by the turnstile. I managed to squeeze my way through in the end, but I still had my full match ticket because the fella behind the turnstile just took his foot off the pedal to let people through to try to alleviate the crush outside.

"That's how I got to see the police open the gate. When I got into the ground I was stood next to it waiting for my mates to come through. But when I saw them about to open it, I realised there was no point standing there as I'd never catch them in the rush of people going past so I went straight down the tunnel into Pen 3. I just thought 'I'll see them back at the coach later on'.

"It was already pretty packed when I got onto the terrace, but I was used to that, having stood on the Kop for years. But it got bad. Much worse than I can ever remember at Anfield. And this happened pretty quickly.

"There's not a lot of me so I managed to navigate myself down towards quite near the front, only a few yards away from the gate. But things were getting worse. People were in trouble. Everyone was screaming at the police to open the gate, but they wouldn't, so people started clambering over the fence. Somehow, I got kind of concertina'd up and somebody grabbed me. They pulled me through the gate, out of the crush.

"I remember falling over onto the track then jumping up and diving back up onto the fence to try and pull people over, but it was virtually impossible to drag them out due to the height of the fence.

"I looked over to the left and saw Liverpool fans pulling down the advertising boards to use as stretchers, so I ran over to try and help them. That's when I came to see Kevin for the first time.

"He was just lying there. I shouted, 'Someone give me a hand with this kid,' and we got him onto an advertising board.

"I didn't even realise there were two policemen and two other fans with me carrying the board. We just ran down to the other end, through the police line, and laid him down on the pitch.

"There was a copper there and I'll never forget what he said to me as I put Kevin down.

"I said to him, 'He needs looking after.' The copper replied, 'He will be, now fuck off back down the other end.'

"We left Kevin with him and went back down to see who else we could help, but I'll never forget what that copper said. He looked at me as if to say, 'This is all your fault'.

"Worst of all, he didn't look after him. Anne found video footage of Kevin lying there on his own before Derek Bruder came down from the stands. Shameful."

Straight away, Mum asked Stevie if he would participate in The Cook Report. He agreed. Within a couple of weeks Stevie got a phone call from the production team to set up an interview with them. It was filmed at the Blundellsands Hotel in Formby. They had a room set up with all their camera equipment and Roger Cook started asking him questions about the day, right from the beginning when they had got off the coach thinking they were simply in Sheffield to watch a football match and go home.

Stevie continues: "That was the first day I'd ever really talked to anyone about it. Anne and my missus were in the room, but I just couldn't do the interview while they were there.

"Roger got onto it and said to them, 'Why don't you two go for a walk down the beach, you can always watch it back later.' They left the room and we got on with it, but it was horrendous for me. Having to go into detail about it all for the first time was incredibly difficult.

"I got everything out, though, and Roger was made up with it as it was so powerful.

"I was in there for a good few hours and when it was done Roger told me to go down to the bar, get myself whatever I wanted and as many as I wanted. It was all on him."

Roger and his crew were fantastic with Mum, with Stevie, with all of us and they were brilliant at their jobs as well. They managed to track down the other two fans that had carried Kevin across the Hillsborough pitch with Stevie.

One of them was a fella called Danny from Skelmersdale. He had phoned Mum on the same evening that the appeal was in the Echo, but wasn't able to tell her anything because he hadn't really looked at Kev while he carried him due to being injured himself.

Danny had broken ribs as well, but was still trying to help people. The same thing was true of many Liverpool fans on the day. They were the heroes of Hillsborough.

The other lad that Cook's team managed to find lived in London, but his brother saw the picture in the Echo and contacted him. He also phoned that night to tell Mum that he thought it might be him, but that he hadn't seen the paper.

His name was Tony O'Keefe, a Liverpool supporting firefighter. His mum had phoned him from Norris Green, saying there was picture in the Echo that looked like him and if it was then he should try to help this Anne Williams lady out.

Mum took the call from Tony and they chatted on the phone for a good while. She was able to confirm exactly what he'd been wearing on the day from the picture. There was no doubt it was Tony and, realising how important it was to her, he told her what had happened on the day.

"I was already working for the fire service in London by 1989," Tony explains, "but travelled back to Liverpool first and then went over to Sheffield with my two brothers and future brother-in-law

"One of my brothers had been to the semi-final the year before and mentioned, as we were walking up to the ground, that it was strange there was no cordon outside like there had been previously, but we didn't realise how bad things were until we got in.

"We were in the upper tier of the Leppings Lane end, in the seating above the terraces, and could soon tell things weren't right. It was clear how unevenly the fans were distributed in the pens below us.

"By the time the fans started coming out of the front of the terrace and were being pulled up into the tier we were in, I remembered I had my camera so I took a few pictures of what was going on.

"I handed those pictures over to the police when I made my statement afterwards, but the only negatives they returned were from shots taken outside Hillsborough before the match.

"It soon became clear that an emergency situation was taking place so, being a firefighter, I made myself known. I was taken downstairs, through the back of the stand, onto the pitch.

"I carried a few people across the pitch on the advertising boards being used as makeshift stretchers. Anne's son Kevin was one of them.

"He was alive, but clearly struggling. I tried to take his pulse when we laid him down at the other end of the pitch, but the police wouldn't let me touch him. One told us, in no uncertain terms, to get back down to the other end.

"I tried to help numerous people with mouth-to-mouth and resuscitation, but there were so many people in need of help and very little assistance from any trained personnel. It was so frustrating to be in that situation as a professional lifesaver and to not have anywhere near adequate equipment to be able to do my job.

"Later on I even managed to get into the gymnasium by the ground that was being used as a makeshift mortuary to try and help.

"Somebody gave me a cup of tea at one point. I was standing outside, trying to drink it, and talking to some police officers. I told them they had got it badly wrong, but they didn't seem interested in what I had to say.

"A priest was there, trying to tell me everything would be alright, and I remember saying to him 'no, it won't be alright.'"

Just as she had done with Stevie, Mum asked Tony if he would be prepared to take part in the TV programme. He agreed. She even travelled down to Streatham, where he lived at the time, with Roger Cook and his film crew to do the piece.

Tony has since said that he thought Mum came across as so driven and so determined to get to the bottom of what had happened. He could tell she was motivated by the deep maternal instincts she felt. Kevin had been taken from her, she'd been lied to and treated terribly, but she just wasn't going to give up and, like Stevie, Tony sensed that and wanted to help.

After doing that interview he kept in touch with Mum and supported her whenever he could because, in his words, "she just had this amazing conviction that the truth would come out eventually. She was right."

You get some strange coincidences in life, like Finlay's birthday being on Truth Day, and in 1994 we'd had another one.

The day The Cook Report into what happened at Hillsborough – they called it 'Kevin's Mum' – was due to be aired just happened to be May 27. It would've been Kev's 21st birthday.

There was going to be a screening for everyone who took part in making the programme at the Blundell-sands Hotel at the same time as The Cook Report was screened across the nation, but with it being Kevin's birthday the decision was made to postpone the programme for almost a week.

Even so, the get-together in Formby still went ahead and everyone had a really good time. Mum felt pleased that the programme had brought a lot of people together, from all over the place, and it gave her a big lift to be able to raise the profile of what she was doing.

Stevie Hart went out the night when it was due to be

shown on television – June 2 – because he didn't know if he could face watching it.

"I set the video to record and thought maybe I'd watch it later on," Stevie continues, "but of course it was on in the pub I went to. Everyone was going 'Look, there's you on the telly' so my decision ended up back-firing a bit. But it was a very good programme. It was really well put together and from then on that was it, me and Anne were mates forever."

Any time Mum had an interview or some media opportunity, she'd send them to see Stevie. With Tony living down south, he was the nearest witness of what happened to Kevin so they stayed really close.

Mum and Stevie did so many interviews. Lots of times they thought she'd cracked it.

Journalists would come out to see them and be blown away by her story, but the published version would be watered down because their legal teams got the jitters.

By now there was never a thought that entered Mum's head that she wouldn't get there in the end.

No-one was allowed to take a backward step. She was adamant that no matter how long it took she would get there in the end and she was absolutely right.

Mum was so steadfast in her belief that it definitely rubbed off on people.

One door would close and she'd say, "Fine, we'll just move onto another one," and keep banging away on the next door.

And the next door. And the one after that.

"It never seemed to get her too down," says Stevie, "or if it did she never showed it. There were times when she'd be disappointed, obviously, but she'd just dust herself down and have another go.

"Anne always seemed to have in mind a different approach she could go for and would get on the phone to me and say, 'Right can you ring such-and-such...' and off we'd go again, bang.

"Her story was so powerful and so laden with the injustice of it all. There was also someone else, a journalist, a radio station or a TV company interested in telling it because of what she was telling them.

"I've seen reporters break down in tears because they were so moved by her story.

"The evidence was so strong that she always used to say to them, 'don't worry about the legal side of it, put it in and let them take me to court.' I think she would have relished that because she had plenty to back herself up with.

"That's what used to get to me. If she was just coming up with these things without such compelling evidence, I could understand up to a point if the media weren't prepared to go with it as it would just be hearsay. But, to have it all there. To know how hard she'd worked to get it. To see it all seemingly going to waste...it was very, very hard to take."

8

Brick Walls

'Anne was so fragile. I just thought, 'How much more can this woman take?'

THE power and impact of doing The Cook Report should never be underestimated.

It shouldn't have needed something like that for it to happen, but it gave Mum's case a lot more credibility.

The programme received a very good reaction when it aired and because the Hillsborough Working Party was still in operation it enabled them to raise various issues.

There was now a lot more flesh on the bones of the story and many people were able to see that there was still so much about Hillsborough that was badly wrong.

It helped towards getting a much greater understanding of the 3.15pm cut-off point and why so many families were unhappy about it.

Kevin was always Mum's priority, but she always felt there may well be other stories just as shocking as his if only the facts could be unearthed.

She got the programme makers to realise this and other families were featured in it as well. I remember Sheila Coleman saying that was symptomatic of how generous Mum was with her evidence.

The Hillsborough Working Party got further publicity in various other parts of the media so it played an invaluable role in helping to push the issue even harder.

Mum got back in touch with her MP, Malcolm Thornton, and he wrote to the Attorney General Nicholas Lyell with the new evidence that she had found.

"The initial response wasn't massively encouraging," Sheila admits, "with him saying Anne could apply for a new inquest again under Section 13 of the Coroner's Act, but it would have to be accompanied by 'significant, cogent and fresh evidence' and he kept making reference to the previous year's judicial review summations, which didn't bode particularly well.

"But Sir Malcolm, as he had become by that point, must have been learning a thing or two from Anne about persistence and he managed to secure a debate in the House of Commons about Kevin's case on November 26, 1994.

"That was a really big moment for Anne. She knew the odds were still stacked against her, but this was an opportunity to have the real story of Hillsborough written into the annals of history for all time, via Hansard, the parliamentary record of all debates, questions and proceedings in Westminster."

Mum was told she didn't necessarily have to be there, but she wouldn't have missed it for the world. She and Sheila travelled down on the afternoon in what they thought would be ample time for the debate, which was not scheduled to start until some time after 9pm.

Sod's law meant they got stuck on the train for hours at Tring because of some problem or other on the line and didn't get into Euston until shortly before it was due to begin.

They had to hurtle across London in a cab and thankfully just about made it in time, meeting up with Tony Edwards, the paramedic found by The Cook Report, who stayed in touch with Mum and had come along to lend his support.

They were given a further reminder, not that it was needed, at just what they were up against when they went through security to get into the Commons that night. "Because of our train delay we hadn't had time to drop our bags at the hotel and, as we were about to go through the scanner, the guard in charge hadn't noticed the small rucksack I had on my shoulder," recalls Sheila.

"I asked if he wanted to check that as well to which he replied, 'Oh watch out, better hide the silver, there's a Scouser in the House.' I remarked to him that it was comments that like which built stereotypes and got people killed, and it underlined yet again the prejudice which informed so much of what had gone on before, during and after Hillsborough.

"Despite that exchange, however, it was a worthwhile exercise. Sir Malcolm was quite clear in his terms of reference and said right from the start it was not his purpose to talk about events from before 3.15pm, which was the whole point.

"He detailed everything that happened to Kevin after that time using the evidence we'd gathered from Derek Bruder, Debra Martin and Tony Edwards and went on to use the reports of the specialist forensic pathologists Dr West and Dr Burns to challenge the medical opinion over Kevin's injuries which Dr Slater had presented to the coroner at the inquests

"He made the point that the newer medical reports had received scant attention at the judicial review and made particular mention of Debra Martin, quite rightly describing the way her evidence had been presented to the jury as "scandalous," quoting directly from a letter Dr Burns had written to Anne:

It strikes me that WPC Martin has been the victim of unjustifiable adverse criticism amounting almost to ridicule.

I am amazed that the evidence of Miss Martin, a Dental Nurse, by training, and a Special Woman Police Constable of five years' standing, is treated with such incredulity, amounting almost to hostility.

From what I have learned from the post-mortem examination of Dr. Slater, and from the evidence given by Dr. Slater at the inquest, I see no reason to doubt the evidence of Miss Martin when she states that she picked Kevin up in her arms, that Kevin opened his eyes, moved his mouth and said 'Mum', flicked his eyelashes, closed his eyes and died.

It meant a lot to Mum to have that moment recorded for posterity so future generations would know the truth about Kevin.

The summing up was just as powerful:

I have spoken to Anne Williams many times and the one thing that impresses most is her desire to know the truth. Somewhere in Sheffield there is a death certificate that relates to Kevin; it does not relate to the circumstances of which Anne Williams is now aware.

In other words, the cut-off point of 3.15pm does not relate to Kevin, and I believe that the evidence shows that clearly.

She has told me more than once that, until the truth is known, neither she nor Kevin will know peace. I believe her.

It is not my purpose, or hers, to expose errors that may have been made that day because of human frailty. That exercise has already been undertaken.

I have already said that I find it difficult to understand why evidence that was freely given was somehow altered afterwards. The purpose is not to point the finger; the purpose is to find out the truth.

I can best finish by quoting Anne Williams.

She said: 'He was just a little boy that went to watch a football match and never came home. There is nothing that I can be told now that will make the agony any worse. I just want to know the truth.'

For those reasons, together with the evidence that I shall certainly give to my Right Hon. and Learned Friend — it will be with his office tomorrow — I urge him to re-examine the case, to exercise the powers available to him under section 13 of the Coroners Act 1988 and to hold a full inquiry.

The House can then show mercy to a family who have suffered for far too long.

Mum and Sheila both found that summing up very moving. Another local MP George Howarth gave a short speech of support and the Attorney General said, while he could not accept a TV programme in itself as evidence, he would examine everything again with an "open mind" if Mum submitted another memorial, although he did keep referring back to the judicial review and why it had come to the verdict it did.

With hindsight, this was indicative of his attitude.

It had gone reasonably well, but Mum and Sheila

knew they were still up against it and needed cheering up so decided to have a little mooch around London before going home.

Sheila takes up the story. "We were by Oxford Street and one of those street auctions was going on.

"Now I normally think they are one of the tackiest things going and anyone who buys anything from them is an idiot. We were saying to each other, 'Look at the state of this lot, I wouldn't spend a penny here, would you trust them?!'

"Before we knew it, we'd spent all our money!

"There was a karaoke machine going for 50 pence and I'd always wanted one of them, and we both got hooked in with this offer of a mystery gift that was being dangled tantalisingly in front of us.

"We were told not to open them until we got outside because otherwise 'everyone will want one'. To this day I still don't know what was wrong with us!

"We went in a doorway nearby to check the 'mystery gifts' out. Anne's was some gaudy-looking necklace and I had this pair of earrings that Bet Lynch wouldn't have been seen dead in.

"At first I said to her, 'Anne, we've got to make a pact, this is between you and I. It goes no further. No-one can ever find out about what idiots we've been. We'll just write it off.'

"But then we got angry, so we went back there and kicked off, asking for our money back.

"Anne ran off at one point and came back with a policeman in tow. They gave us our money back – eventually – but I still didn't trust them so we made them
take us to a bank. Sure enough, the notes were fakes.

"They kept saying 'give us the karaoke machine
back,' but there was no way they were getting it.

"They gave us a bit of stick as we were leaving so
Anne turned around and said, 'Don't you speak to me
like that, I know Roger Cook and I'm going to tell him
all about you!'

"I was laughing hysterically by the time we turned the
corner and that became our little catchphrase all the
way home, 'I'll get Roger Cook onto you!'"

Mum set about preparing the memorial for the Attorney General and George came up with a tremendous recommendation, pointing her in the direction of
Elkan Abrahamson.

He became her new solicitor and a wonderful supporter of the fight for justice, giving countless hours of
his time and expertise for free.

Mum's detective skills enabled her to notice a fairly
significant error when she was again going through
her files from the judicial review. She left nothing to
chance.

The 'form 99' which she found in the bundle referred
to which part of the body of the deceased had been
injured, and in this case said 'chest' rather than 'neck'.

This was important because the traumatic asphyxia

cause of death, which she disputed so vociferously, was caused by compression of the chest whereas Mum had gone to all this trouble to prove that Kevin's death was actually caused by broken bones in his neck, which had caused him to suffocate.

The expert opinion she gathered now told her that you couldn't die from traumatic asphyxia with a neck injury so she went about getting Dr Slater to amend the form from 'chest' to 'neck'.

He did that, eventually, but refused to provide a new report for the forthcoming memorial taking into account the new medical evidence she had found, sending her a nasty letter saying how saddened he was to hear that expert forensic pathology opinions had been sought "behind his back."

While waiting for the Attorney General to come back with his answer, Jimmy McGovern came on the scene wanting to make a TV docu-drama about Hillsborough.

Mum spent a lot of time with Jimmy talking to his researchers about the evidence in Kevin's case. He wanted to run Kevin's case as one of the main stories in the programme.

Jimmy had already devoted an episode of Cracker to a Hillsborough storyline a couple of years earlier and Mum was very keen to do it, but was in a very difficult position because of the legal avenue she was still pursuing to get Kevin's inquest reopened.

She spoke at length with her MP and the various legal people involved, but the advice was that taking part in the TV drama would not be looked upon favourably and could jeopardise her case.

So Mum reluctantly had to ring Jimmy and tell him that although he could blast Kevin's case all over the media, he couldn't give her the new inquest she wanted so she couldn't go ahead with it.

She helped with some of the research, but felt she had let him down, even though Sheila, and plenty of others, all told her she hadn't let anyone down.

To compound things, eight months before the programme was due to be shown, the Attorney General's office rejected her memorial anyway, again saying it was "not in the interests of justice." That just made her feel worse.

The Labour party getting back into power after 18 years soon afterwards, however, gave Mum and our supporters renewed hope.

The McGovern drama aired in December 1996 and Labour had campaigned locally, for the following May's general election, promising to look into Hillsborough. The new Home Secretary Jack Straw announced soon after taking office that an independent judicial scrutiny would be set up to examine new evidence.

Sheila continues: "Anne, George and I used to go up to Straw's constituency in Blackburn quite a bit because there was a solicitor there who helped us and we felt very optimistic that Labour would back up their words with action.

"Even after all the setbacks to that point, we still took things at face value.

"But from the minute the man in charge, Lord Justice Stuart-Smith, turned up at the Albert Dock on October 6, 1997 and made his now infamous, but still quite staggering, 'Have you got a few of your people or are they like the Liverpool fans, turn up at the last minute?' quip to the waiting families, it was clear that another whitewash was on the cards."

As ever, Mum was prepared to try to give Stuart-Smith the benefit of the doubt. She sent him a four-page letter in addition to all her evidence.

Sheila went with her to meet him at the Maritime Museum and it was clear that he knew her case was different to the others. However, he already seemed to be trying to palm her off, asking if she would be satisfied with a report establishing what had happened to Kevin after 3.15pm if he couldn't recommend a fresh inquest or new judicial inquiry?

Sheila explains how it went. "Anne knew she was getting the thin end of the wedge and laid it down to him straight:

'I know what happened to Kevin after 3.15pm.

'I've tracked everybody down, I've spoken to everybody who was with him.

'I've spent hours with forensic pathologists. I know why he died and Dr Slater was mistaken about Kevin's injuries in the inquest court.

'If you look at that body file in front of you, you'll see a picture of my dead son in a body bag.

'You can see on it that he is not blue and bloated. He looks haunted, but he is not how Dr Slater said he was at the inquest.

'I said goodbye to my son and there wasn't a mark on him.'

"She had had her say at least, but Stuart-Smith's demeanour as we left, staring out the window with his back to us, spoke volumes."

Mum was pleased that Derek Bruder had volunteered himself to give evidence in person and that did give her her some hope.

However, when they travelled down to London again the following February, it all felt painfully familiar, sitting there in room 13 of the House of Commons to hear Jack Straw tell them there was nothing he could do

They had been stitched up again. It was awful.

Sheila carries on: "I felt for everyone affected, of course, but Anne was so fragile. I just thought 'How much more can this woman take?'

"She would go on real downers, but she would always come back for more because she loved her son. She knew what happened to him was not right, she had the evidence to prove it and she was just not going to give up.

"There is no doubt that the case of Kevin Williams became very high profile at times within the context of Hillsborough. This is because the nature and extent of the cover up in Kevin's case is massive, yet Anne always maintained that there may be other cases where the facts are equally, or even more, disturbing."

Mum worked extremely hard, not just in scouring any means available to find evidence and any nuggets of information that she could use, but also in using every media opportunity she could to highlight the various injustices and the positive role played by survivors who were still being blamed in some quarters.

She came in for a lot of criticism from other families. Some said she was only concerned with Kevin's case. Others were downright horrible to her at times.

What they could never see was that she was pushing it forward all the time and that Kevin's case could be critical to all the other ones, which of course it proved to be.

She would often say that she was lucky in a way because at least she knew what had happened to her son, whereas so many other families had been left in the dark.

This 'luck' was obtained though from an awful lot of legwork, done while she was still trying to cope with the heartbreaking loss of her son. My brother.

Mum and Sheila trekked to all kinds of places to basically beg for whatever information they could get.

She wasn't afraid to approach people from completely different walks of life and between the two of them they found ways to uncover what had gone on behind the scenes with Hillsborough. It was a national disgrace.

Her supporters could never fail to be moved by the tenacity of her desire to see justice for Kevin, but what they didn't know was that away from her Hillsborough campaigning, Mum's life was far from easy, something she wrote about in the months before she passed away.

The following chapter is written in Mum's words.

It's important to remember that this is the book she wanted to write. This is the part of Mum's story that only her family and closest friends knew.

It's a story she wanted to tell...

9

From The Heart
*'My new life was not all that I had
hoped for... I was so unhappy'*

'STEVE was a wonderful father to Sara, Michael and
Kevin, and brought the two boys up as his own, but
sadly our marriage was unable to survive the strain that
Hillsborough put on it and we split up in 1995.

We had been married for 18 years and gone through
a lot together, but it became very difficult for us to com-
municate after losing Kevin. The first six months were
very tough, but I had the campaign to keep me occu-
pied and gradually got on with my life.

Getting justice for Kevin was my driving force. He always had such a strong sense of right and wrong, even

as a young boy. He would have been very angry with what happened over Hillsborough. I always kept that in mind.

The continued knock-backs from the Attorney General and the Stuart-Smith stitch-up were very, very frustrating, but I knew from quite early on that Kevin was the awkward little boy who did not fit neatly into the 3.15pm cut-off point.

That was what kept letting the guilty off the hook and stopped any questions from being asked about the lack of care afterwards. Kevin only needed fairly basic medical attention to have survived and if that was the case for him, then how many of the others could have been saved?

I knew that was why they didn't want to give me a new inquest. It would've opened up a can of worms. They were scared of where it could lead. What the repercussions could be. That a thorn in their side would turn out to be a branch full of them.

It felt like they were trying to wear me down, but my attitude was 'I'll wear them down before they wear me down'.

So I kept going.

I met someone and moved to Chester to be with him. I missed Sara and Michael very much, but I would travel back to Formby once a week to make sure they were alright.

Legally, there didn't seem to be anywhere to go, but

I kept involved with what was going on as the Hillsborough Justice Campaign began to get underway and I had some peace of mind knowing I had done everything I could think of for Kevin.

I still wanted a new inquest, though, because there was no way I was going to pick up his death certificate until it had the right information on it. I was adamant about that.

Everyone kept saying it was the end of the legal road after the Stuart-Smith stitch-up. The private prosecutions against Murray and Duckenfield in 2000, which were another whitewash, showed the doors to justice were still locked tight.

I managed to get a book published telling the story of my fight for Kevin and that made me happy because it enabled people to read the truth about what really happened to him and us as we tried to clear the names of the 96 and all our survivors.

I got lots of lovely letters from mothers who had read it, telling me not to give up. It helped to know that people cared, people I'd never met and who didn't know me. Such things strengthened my resolve. It was wonderful to have such support.

My new life in Chester was not all I that hoped for, though. Unfortunately, my partner was drinking heavily.

It started off a couple of times a week and then he started bringing home a bottle of Scotch most nights.

My heart used to sink when I saw him coming up the path with a carrier bag full of booze as I knew it would be another horrible night as he got more and more drunk.

The verbal abuse was appalling. Then it started to turn physical.

I was so unhappy. I didn't really know anyone in Chester, so I had no-one to turn to.

When he was sober he was the nicest man you could wish to meet, but when he was drunk he was different altogether.

Steve and I had split up because we could not relate to the death of Kevin. We couldn't talk about it.

This was different. I had never been treated so badly in all my life, but I had no-one to confide in about what was happening so I just carried on for a while, hoping that he would go back to being the man I had moved in with.

But things just kept getting worse. I used to go to bed to keep out of his way, but even then he wouldn't leave me alone, dragging me out of bed and trying to throw me out of the flat. The police were always coming around and I would get the blame for ringing them when it would have been one of the neighbours.

I was devastated at how things had turned out. I could not understand why this man had changed so much.

I used to ask him, "What have I done?" and all he would say is, "You know what you've done."

He gave me no answers.

Then he started staying out at night. I never knew when he was coming back or what state he would be in if he did.

One Friday he didn't come home so I put all his clothes in bin bags outside the front door.

When he returned the following morning he was not very pleased. He dragged all his clothes in and threw them in the spare room before going out again.

The following day he came back, packed his car with his stuff and left. He told me he was going to stay with one of his brothers. I was so relieved because I just could not live like that anymore.

I still hoped he might get himself sorted out. I could not understand how two people could live in the same flat and not speak, but whenever I asked him what his problem was he would just ignore me. It was a terrible way to live.

A week later I found out that he had moved in with another woman on the estate. I was shocked. I never even thought he might be seeing someone else. I just saw the problem of his drinking.

I contacted a women's group for battered wives and started to meet them on a Friday.

When I told the group he had gone, one of them came with me to the Chester Housing Trust because he paid the rent and I was just on sick money, which was not much.

I was in for another shock when the council told me to give them the keys back. The flat was in his name so they were saying I had to get out. I couldn't believe what I was hearing.

We went to see a welfare solicitor, Martin Tucker, who was very helpful, thankfully. I explained my situation and right away he rang the housing trust to tell them that I was classed as his common-law wife and they would have to take me to court to get me out.

He helped me fill out the forms to claim housing rebate and told me to go home and not worry about losing the flat.

The funny thing was that being on my own meant more of the neighbours started to speak to me so I realised they had known what was going on. It must have been them who had called the police, fearing for me.

Some time later, I found out that my ex-partner had hit the woman he was living with and knocked her teeth out.

I had a lucky escape. That could have been me.

It was a tough time. I was upset that I had given everything up to start a new life and now I was left in Chester worrying whether I was going to lose my home or not.

Sara had asked me to go back home, but there was not enough room as she had got into a relationship and had my first granddaughter, Lena.

I didn't feel I could go back to Formby so I decided

to make a life for myself in Chester. The housing trust eventually signed the flat over to me so I felt a lot more secure and Karen, my next door neighbour, asked me would I like to go out for a drink with her and her friends.

Gradually, I was getting my life back. I was going out and meeting new people. Things were improving.

My children, Michael and Sara, have had to live with Hillsborough and with me fighting the British legal system for nearly their whole lives.

They both accepted it and supported me as they knew I had to do it for Kevin.

Sara was more interested than Michael in the things I was doing, perhaps because she was the youngest. The boys were six and eight when she was born and she was close to both of them.

Michael had always said to me, "I know what you are doing and I know you have to do it for our Kevin, but I don't want to know the details." That was fair enough in my opinion. He supported me and that was all I wanted. I did not want Hillsborough to ruin their lives, losing their brother was bad enough.

Hillsborough was a huge part of my life, but if I went down a legal avenue I would close it off for a bit while I was waiting for an answer. I had to try and focus on other aspects of my life as well.

I was quite happy knowing I was doing something

about the injustice in Kevin's case, even if the knock-backs were upsetting with the evidence clearly there, but still getting ignored.

I knew what I was up against and how powerful the Establishment was, but it just made me more determined to carry on.

I was not going to let them brush Kevin under the carpet. He might have been worth nothing to the system, but he meant the world to me.

My two brothers, Danny and Christopher, as well as my children, helped keep me going. Every time we had a press release, a little success or one of the many knock-backs, they would ring me up to let me know they were still on my side.

The sad thing was I had never been close to my mother or sister. There was always some disagreement or another and it did not take much for them not to talk to me. It could go on for a year or a few months and then we would speak again until the next incident.

Sara was to become the next reason we had a fall out. She was in a bad relationship and became pregnant.

My mother and sister were not happy about it and neither was I but there was nothing I could do. I was excited that I was going to have a grandchild even though the circumstances could have been better.

What upset me was once again the lack of support from my mother and sister. They told me that I should get on with my life. They kept saying Sara had made her bed and should be left to lie in it, in other words "wash your hands of her and the baby."

I could not believe it and said to my mother one day, "I have already lost one child, I am not going to lose another".

When Lena was finally born, I was over the moon. She was so lovely and Sara was so happy, but my mother and sister did not bother with her. They didn't even speak to Sara, so we fell out once again.

Sara is a great mum, and the relationship she was in only lasted until Lena was about eight months old. That's when she split from her partner.

She would bring Lena to Chester for the weekends and I enjoyed having them around so much. Being a grandparent is so rewarding. Michael and his partner had a little girl, Grace, a few years later and she is adorable as well.

Finlay came along shortly afterwards and there's so much of Kevin in him. He's very clever and very loving, just like his uncle was. Every so often he gives you a certain look and I just think, 'Oh my God, that's Kevin'.

He is so very like him.'

Anne

10

Two Lives

'I don't think she truly realised how important she was to other people'

MUM ended up with two separate lives in the end. She taught herself how to keep Hillsborough removed from everything else.

One minute you'd be with your mother, the next you were with this fiercely determined woman who wanted to take on the world to get justice for her son. It was kind of surreal.

Being able to split things apart like that meant that she was able to completely throw herself into things when she was in 'work mode,' so much so that it was funny at times.

I remember hearing her ring up Sheila Coleman once and she'd been gabbing away for what must have been the best part of ten minutes before going, "Anyway, give me a ring, love, when you get this message."

She'd been talking to an answer machine the whole time.

Mum used to do it to me as well. I remember being with a mate once and listening to the voicemail message back, laughing our heads off. The thing is, the message was so long I used up all my credit listening to it so I couldn't phone her back!

That's just how Mum was. She was completely devoted to her grandchildren, to me and Michael, and enjoyed spending time with her friends, going out at the weekend.

It must have been difficult given how involved she was, but some days she would just close herself off to Hillsborough. Even when she was putting notes together to write her next book.

If she didn't feel like doing anything on it then she just wouldn't turn the computer on. She'd switch off. Go and do something else instead. It must have been the only way she could stay sane.

As time went on, she was able to keep her grief and Hillsborough separate as well, which must be hard for some people to understand.

When we'd go to the annual memorial services at Anfield and sit on the Kop, I'd be in bits, but Mum had learned to remove her feelings about Kevin away from the work she was doing. It showed how strong she could be.

She would get upset privately and would quietly shed a tear or two and say a few prayers.

I don't think she ever truly realised how important she was to other people.

At the 20th anniversary service at Anfield there was a woman who lost her son at the 1971 Ibrox disaster. 66 Rangers supporters were killed, and over 200 injured, through crush injuries sustained after somebody fell in a stairwell during celebrations after a last minute equaliser in a game against Celtic.

This lady chased after Mum and told her "keep going." Having lost her own son at a football match 38 years earlier she could empathise with what Mum was going through. For someone to come to Anfield to speak to her and wish her well in her fight for justice spurred Mum on again.

So too did the many letters she got from people all over the world. Ordinary people, mums and dads who had heard about what she was doing and why she was doing it. They gave her added strength.

Sheila has told me how Mum's name has cropped up several times in some of the work she has been involved with on fighting injustice, in completely different areas to Hillsborough, simply because of the way she just refused to give up and challenged authority.

Mum always used to say it was the Liverpool supporters who kept her going, but when I used to tell her what
a lift she gave the survivors she thought I was talking
daft!

Maybe in the last couple of years, she started to twig
a bit. We'd be going in The Albert pub before a home
match and people would be calling her name. "Anne,
Anne, come and sit here girl," as we walked in. But,
even though people would tell her, I don't think she
fully understood the impact that she had.

One person who did understand and appreciate
Mum's importance was Peter Carney, a Liverpool supporter and Hillsborough campaigner who had been in
Pen 3 on April 15, 1989. His story shows just what an
impact Mum had.

Peter's story...

'It's impossible to underestimate how important Anne's
support was to the survivors.

It was massive. She had a humility and a gentleness
to her that said, 'I may have lost my son but don't you
be feeling guilty,' and that's why I held her close. Other
bereaved victims said similar, but Anne had a genuine
understanding and empathy for the suffering of survivors. I am one of them.

I owe my life to the actions of Liverpool supporters
that day.

I've been an avid Liverpool fan all my life. My wife Tina discovered she was pregnant about 10 days before Hillsborough and I was about to turn 30.

On the day of the match, it was beautifully bright and sunny. We all agreed with Bill Shankly's quote about FA Cup semi-final day being the best of the season and we couldn't wait for the big game, with Wembley hopefully beckoning again.

Our group of five split up, so just two of us headed for Pen 3 in the Leppings Lane end.

As we shuffled into this pitch-black, eight-foot wide tunnel, there was a surge where the level ground became a steep slope causing a momentum that forced us forward.

The force was so great I entered the terrace with my back to the pitch, facing the tunnel I had just gone through. The pen was jam-packed with people, all moving. As I tried to find my feet and face the pitch, there was another surge, and another. I saw people had fallen to the ground in front of me and heard people screaming.

The game had just started and I could feel myself being crushed as the pressure felt more and more intense. I tried to stay on my feet and gain a bit of space, but I couldn't raise my arms and my feet could barely touch the floor.

Then, my chest felt tighter and tighter as I found it harder to breathe. People at the front were screaming at the police to let them out and I joined in, yelling at the top of my voice, but they ignored us. I saw one man trying to climb over the fence, then be pushed back into the pen by the police.

I was terrified. I gave up screaming for help, trying to conserve what air I had left in my lungs. I lost the sensation in my legs, which went numb. I couldn't feel anything waist downwards. All the pressure was on my chest, my breath getting harder and harder to keep up. I tilted my head back and up to find air and saw the man beside me dying, his face changing colour. As I struggled to breathe, I thought I was about to die.

I made a conscious effort to distract myself from the crush, looking at the players on the pitch and the stands on different sides of the ground. I thought I was waist high to other people's shoulders, grasping for air.

I remember looking higher and higher up, towards the sky and the clouds, then had a near death experience. My vision travelled down a 'cloud tube' then I watched myself from on high, being crushed in the middle of a perfect circle of people, my head was shoulder high to those around me.

My last conscious thought was 'What about Tina, Tina and the baby'. Then everything went black.

My first sensation after this was of my torso being thumped. I think I was passed back, face down, over the top of the crowd. Then I felt as if my limbs were being stretched, my vision was black and I can hear an echoing noise. I think this was Liverpool supporters carrying me back through the tunnel.

I came around at the back of the stadium by the turnstiles. My first conscious thought was 'I'm here, I'm here'.

My first conscious vision was of a red brick wall. It was blurred. Then I saw three coppers stood in front of a dead man with a bare, bloated belly and his denim jacket draped over his head.

My friend, Mike, came out of Pen 3 and saw me lying on the floor. He shook my right shoulder and I told him "don't touch me, I am aching all over." He had me moved to the wall of the stand and I was taken to hospital.

I was X-rayed and examined and allowed to leave about 7pm. As soon as we got into the car the news came on the radio. They announced that 93 people were dead. We were left totally dumbstruck, switched the radio off and drove home in silence.

My near-death experience at Hillsborough became a pivotal part of my life and nothing felt normal any more. I went back to the stadium a few times to pay tribute to the dead, acutely aware of surviving an almighty threat to my existence.

It took me months to sleep properly at night and I was on sick leave for six months from my job as a play development worker. Sometimes I would lose my temper for no reason, or cry incessantly.

I started attending a self-help survivor's group, organised through social services, each week. When my son, Thomas, was born, he was such a good focus. The first time he went out of the house, at the official opening of the Hillsborough Centre, he was in the arms of Kenny Dalglish. I felt blessed again. I felt I could work again.

But for a few years afterwards, I was in a mess trying to get my head around what happened, trying to grasp how lucky I'd been and working out ways of repaying what I owed to the supporters who saved my life.

Me and mates made a banner, from material I was saving to use for an LFC Centenary celebration banner, the week after the disaster. We wrote the names of those who had died on the trophies that Liverpool had won, and hung it on the corner of Anfield Road and Kemlyn Road.

I vowed there and then that the banner would be a living memorial to those that were killed. I lived and so the banner, with the names and memories of those who were killed, should live too.

Anne's end goal was, of course, to achieve justice for Kevin and for the 96, but what she constantly strove to do and what distinguished her from everyone else was that she went out of her way to tell people the true story of what happened.

I knew what Anne said about survivors and how their role saving and trying to save lives was spot on. That was the glue that held us together.

I felt so close to her because we were two sides of the same coin, I suppose.

I helped her understand the situation Kevin had been in and the investigative work she did helped me understand the situation I had been in. I knew that what happened to Kevin could have happened to me, and vice versa.

There's only one difference between survivors and the 96. We all went into those pens together. Some of us came out alive and some of us, as we know and will never forget, didn't. But we're the same. That bond is always with us.

It may sound strange, but if you could take me back and ask me where I'd want to be if we were to go through it all again I'd say "right there in the middle, but I come out alive," which is what I did, so that I knew exactly what happened, exactly what we went through. The physical pain. The mental despair. The desperate fight for breath and life.

When I saw Dr John Ashton on the TV in the days afterwards, telling the world what had happened, I recognised him from the rescue behind the stand and knew he was absolutely right, but nobody wanted to listen to him.

Anne had this encyclopaedic grasp of the nuances, terminology and medical detail for what happened to many of the 96 and the circumstances surrounding their deaths.

She could identify other cases, often by a small snip-
pet of information, and probably would have been
able to name quite a few of those who the Independent
Panel said could've been saved, off the top of her head.

She told me the doctor that did Kevin's autopsy carried out 16 in about two hours. If that's one every ten
minutes or so, how properly were they actually being
done?

The fella must have been on roller-skates. And she
could reel lots of them off. 'This doctor did this one,
this doctor did that one, this doctor did the other one,
and so on.'

Her insight, not just into Kevin's movements and the
chain of events on the day, but also the medical evidence around traumatic asphyxia and conventional asphyxia made a big impact on me because the process of
death described in the reports she obtained was exactly
what I went through. Except for one thing. I woke up.

With just a little bit more assistance how many others
could have been saved?

Kevin only needed oxygen or a tracheotomy, but
there were others who didn't even need that much.

I knew it was Tina and the baby that had kept me
alive so my guilt at having survived was mixed with this
feeling of being blessed with the best that life can offer.

I had to talk about what I went through and deal with
it that way. Some other survivors weren't able to do
that, though.

They couldn't cope with what they'd experienced, how it was being dealt with and how they'd been treated, so more lives were lost and destroyed.

One survivor wanted unions on strike, factories closed, buses stopped, the country brought to a standstill. He was found dead in a garden shed the day after watching a Hillsborough documentary on television. His political analysis was spot on.

I've always said, "there's 101 dead and 101 things to do in their name" and I've lived that. That's how I've dealt with things, helping survivors to try and carry on because I needed their help to carry on. To realise where we'd been, what had been done to us, where we were going, and what we could do for each other.

Where the Hillsborough Justice Campaign and Anne were so important was that they enabled people to feel they could help each other. Discuss things they were going through, because clearly significant numbers of people didn't feel able to do that for a long time.

The main insight that I got into what happened and needed to happen was through John Glover, who had lost his son, Ian, at Hillsborough and had two other sons, Joe and John, who were survivors.

Poor Joe was particularly badly affected, sometimes being found sleeping on his brother's grave in Kirkdale cemetery. He was tragically killed ten years after Hillsborough, crushed by marble slabs in a work accident after he bravely pushed a colleague out of the way.

I got to know John senior through the self-help groups at the Hillsborough Centre and became friendly with him and his family. We were founder members of the HJC. When John died in Easter week, 2013, I made a banner that said,

JOHN 4:96.

I call it my biblical banner.

After the Stuart-Smith stitch-up, some families wanted a different approach to the one the Hillsborough Family Support Group was taking.

Many people continued to feel there was an urgent need for survivors to be part of things so that's how the HJC came into being. Also, some survivors had won professional negligence legal actions against their solicitors, which was significant in showing we had not been properly represented.

It was originally called the Hillsborough Relatives, Survivors and Supporters Association. I was the founding chairman and worked with the group for a long time.

Anybody who was having difficulties, or wanted to talk to a survivor, spoke to me.

The deal was: I'll listen to you, if you listen to me.

It wasn't counselling in a social worker way, it was more about mutual support.

It was an unusual way of dealing with disaster and trauma because usually the people involved in that kind of situation have little in common, before or after,

but we were different in that we were all Liverpool supporters as well, one and the same, before and after.
That's what I had always got out of being a Liverpool
supporter.

It's a community. Our community. A family.

Anne wasn't directly involved right at the start, but
came on board with us not long afterwards and became
chairman for a few years. I was aware of her because of
her petitions to the Attorney General and involvement
in the judicial review of the inquests.

One of the things that always struck me about Anne's
work in the early years was the help she got from her
MP, Sir Malcolm Thornton, which straight away made
me think she must have something about her if she
managed to get a Tory involved!

During the first conversation I had with her, she gave
me down the banks because I hadn't read her book.
I knew of Kevin's rescue and trusted her to be right
about the conspiracy to cover it up.

One of the key things about the HJC was to broaden
the perspective of things so that families were involved
and survivors were included as well.

Survivors had no collective or organised voice before
this. Yet our experiences on the day, and since, are so
important to the sense of injustice felt throughout the
city.

There was a whole load of damage done that hadn't
been recognised, and as well as that, survivors were in

the important position of being able to shed a lot of light to add to the families' understanding of what had happened, by virtue of their experiences outside the ground and in the pens.

Without Anne, though, things would have been very different.

As I said, it should never be underestimated just how important her support was to all the Hillsborough survivors.'

Peter Carney

Dave Kirby, a well known Liverpool supporting writer and playwright, also got to know Mum. He first met her through Peter Carney, who he went to school with, and the work they were doing for the Hillsborough Justice Campaign.

He was another Hillsborough survivor who struggled to deal with his emotions about that day.

Dave never used to be able to talk about Hillsborough at all, even to his wife or to his brothers, who were there with him on the day.

But, gradually, he was able to write about it, something he admits helped him, and when he learned that other people got some comfort from that as well he got more involved in the campaign.

Mum loved Dave's writing and she had quite an impact on him.

Dave's story...

'When I was doing performance art of the Hillsborough poems I'd written in the early years of my involvement, there would be healthy crowds of a few hundred in the Masque theatre. But after a while, they had dwindled away. One night in the Croxteth British Legion there were about 14 people there.

There was very much a feeling of 'how much further can we go?' And if we were thinking that, how must the families have been feeling? It must have been hard for them to believe they were ever going to get any sort of truth or justice from a system that had completely betrayed them.

Anne kept things going and that was very important to a lot of people. Many were clinging to the fact that she was still battling away and hoped she would get somewhere with it as it could open things up for everyone else.

From the first time I met her, I was blown away by the passion of the woman. A lot of people felt there was nowhere left to go, but she just wasn't having it.

When you met Anne, you could see the pain in her eyes straight away. It was almost like she was looking through you at times, but I knew about the journey she was on.

She was so passionate and fiercely intelligent, but so filled with pain as well. Even my wife remarked on it one time when she met her. "You can see the pain in that poor woman's eyes," she said. But you could feel it as well.

Anne was angry because, unlike a lot of the families, she knew the truth of what had happened to Kevin from witness accounts. The authorities knew that his sequence of events didn't fit in with the 3.15pm cut-off point so Anne became a problem and was consequently treated appallingly, which made her acutely aware of the scale of the cover-up to hide the truth.

I often used to think of her in those darker times when she would have been on her own in her flat and it seemed like there was never going be any kind of breakthrough.

There didn't seem to be any light at the end of that tunnel. How did she keep going, where did she go on those nights?

It was amazing, on this incredible crusade that she was on, that she managed to stay sane, but somehow she did. Anne stayed true to herself as well.

I got to know Anne more over the years and she'd always amaze me because she had this incredible ability to pick you up when you were feeling low.

I'd often get flashbacks to the day itself when we'd be sitting around talking about how things were going and it could be very difficult sometimes, but she would always be the one to bring people a bit of hope when it should've been the other way around!

Anne must have cried a million tears, but none of us ever saw them. She always carried herself with the utmost dignity and epitomised everything good about our fantastic city. The fight, the pride, the rebellious-ness, the resilience, the love.

Her ability to just keep going was an inspiration to me because I had gone through a bad time myself after my own experience at Hillsborough.

It led to me write a poem called the 'The Justice Bell,' which I did back in 2002.

It was about a young lad who sat opposite me on the coach journey to the match that day.

I spoke to him quite a lot on the way there. He was a lovely, well-mannered, well-spoken boy who idolised John Barnes. The last thing he said to me was: "Three nil – Barnesie hat-trick." We shook hands and he went on his way. Little did any of us know what was about to unfold.

What I witnessed and heard that day has scarred me for life.

In the aftermath, we were waiting on the coach listen-ing to the harrowing death count rising by the minute. The young boy's seat stayed empty.

The coach eventually headed to the ground to find out if they had a list of missing names, but such was the chaos at the stadium that extracting information was impossible.

It was getting to dusk by this time – the surreal sight

of hundreds of blue emergency lights silently flashing will always remain vivid.

A decision was taken to return home without the boy.

We came back over the moors, which were absolutely pitch black, and I was constantly drawn to the empty seat opposite me. I prayed so hard for that kid to be safe.

We were the very last coach home returning to Anfield at 11pm that night and I remember a lone scarf was tied to the Shankly Gates. It was an Everton scarf.

The next morning I got a phone call telling me that the young boy had been killed. It cut me in half.

The year before, in 1988, we had a really bad time in the fatal Pen 3, so in 1989 all of us – 17 lads – made a pre-match pact not to go near the central pens and head to the side pen by the corner flag.

That pact undoubtedly saved some of us from being killed that day.

For years afterwards, and occasionally even still today, I have nightmares. I often dream that I'm on the coach telling the lad not to go down the tunnel. Then I wake up, laden with guilt.

On the 10th anniversary, in 1999, I remember reading an interview with one of the bereaved mothers who said that her son's bedroom had never been touched since the tragedy.

It was that image, and my own experience, which inspired The Justice Bell poem.

I've always kept the boy's identity a secret as lots of the bereaved families have told me that they feel like my poem was written for them. Anne Williams was one of them.

Of all my successes in theatre and film, or indeed anything I've ever written, my proudest moment undoubtedly came at the Hillsborough memorial service at Anfield in 2002 when I saw Anne and Sara wearing t-shirts with a picture of Kevin and my Justice Bell poem.

To help bring a bit of comfort to someone who has been dealt such a really bad hand in life was very important to me.

They started selling them in the HJC shop, so I'd often see people with them on at the match for years afterwards.

THE JUSTICE BELL

A schoolboy holds a leather ball
In a photograph on a bedroom wall
The bed is made, the curtains drawn
As silence greets the break of dawn.

The dusk gives way to morning light
Revealing shades of red and white
Which hang from posters locked in time
Of the Liverpool team of '89.

Sara Williams

Upon a pale white quilted sheet
With a yellow scarf, trimmed with red
And some football boots beside the bed.
A football kit is folded neat.

In hope, the room awakes each day
To see the boy who used to play
But once again it wakes alone
For this young boy's not coming home.

Outside…the springtime fills the air
The smell of life is everywhere
Violas bloom and tulips grow
While daffodils dance heel to toe.

These should have been such special times
For a boy who'd now be in his prime
But spring forever turned to grey
In the Yorkshire sun that April day.

The clock was locked on 3.06
As sun shone down upon the pitch
Lighting faces etched in pain
As death descended on Leppings Lane.

Between the bars an arm is raised
Amidst a human tidal wave
A body too frail to fight for breath
Is drowned below a sea of death.

With Hope In Her Heart

His outstretched arm then disappears
To signal twenty four years of tears
As 96 souls of those who fell
Await the toll of the justice bell.

Ever since that tragic day
A vision often comes my way
I reach and grab his outstretched arm
Then pull him up away from harm.

I hear his voice, I see his face
But wishful dreams are soon replaced
By the vision that haunts me most
An empty seat on a silent coach.

On April the 15th every year
When all is calm and skies are clear
Beneath a glowing Yorkshire moon
A lone Scot's piper plays a tune.

The tune rings out the justice cause
Then blows due west across the moors
It passes by the eternal flame
Then engulfs a young boy's picture frame.

His room is as it was that day
For twenty four years it's stayed that way
Untouched and frozen forever in time
Since that terrible day in '89.

Sara Williams

And as the pipes play their haunting sound
Tears are heard from miles around
They're tears from the families of those who fell
Still awaiting the toll of the justice bell.

Dave Kirby

11

My Red Family

*'Grown men cried. This 5ft 5in mother
had turned into their leader'*

DESPITE constantly being told that there wasn't another legal avenue to go down, Mum's resolve didn't waver. Having met so many survivors, fellas like Peter Carney and Dave Kirby, and heard their horrific stories, she knew she had to keep on exploring different options. Continue the fight. Not just for Kev, but for them all.

Making the truth known about what happened to Kev and getting justice for him was at the forefront of her mind, but so too was stopping those who had caused the Hillsborough disaster – and been complicit in the subsequent cover-up – from getting away with it.

As far as Mum was concerned, the more people that knew about what really happened at Hillsborough, the more chance she had of being successful. It was something she wrote about herself.

Mum's words...

'Kevin's evidence was already so strong and I kept adding to it little by little, sometimes only minor details, but it all increased the weight of my argument.

It was important to keep telling people about Hillsborough and the cover-up as well. Why should they be allowed to get away with it?

My attitude was the more people that knew about it, the better. They could one day help to make the difference. So I would travel to places and talk to groups of people or appear on TV and radio chat shows if I was asked to.

I would be quite happy if I ended a day with the knowledge that one more person knew the truth.

Then, in 2005, my barrister contacted me to say a new ruling had come out from the European Court of Human Rights which could relate to Kevin's case.

They had brought in an amendment to article 2 – 'the right to life' – and because Kevin had died in the hands of the state he was entitled to a full inquiry into how he died and what he died from. It was a possible breakthrough. A way out of the legal cul-de-sac I'd gone down.

Because of the 3.15pm cut-off point and all the lies that were told at Kevin's mini inquests, such questions had never been properly answered. This, potentially, would change that.

It was the first legal option I'd had in quite a while, but I was told I would have to wait at least two years before I would get an answer. It also became clear that we would first have to go through this country, with another submission to the Attorney General under Section 13 of the Coroners Act, before we could get anywhere near the European Court.

If he turned us down again, for the third time, then we could actually submit to Europe.

I thought about it for a while. Could I go through a two year process just to be told again that I don't have a case? I had to. I realised that if I didn't do it I would never know the outcome.

Europe could have the power to give me a new inquest and I couldn't let that opportunity, whether it was likely or not, to slip through my fingers. 2005 was the year of an unlikely European victory for Liverpool so maybe events in Istanbul would be a good omen.

The first thing we had to do was to get another draught from Edward Fitzgerald QC so we could build the evidence to submit to the Attorney General. Once again, he very kindly offered his services for free.

I also needed more medical advice from Dr Iain West who had done numerous reports for me on Kevin.

I rang Guy's Hospital in London to make an appointment with Dr West, but I was in for an almighty shock. His secretary told me that he had died.

I was so upset. Completely taken aback. Dr West had spent hours with me over the years. I had so much trust and respect for him. I cried on the end of the phone.

Sue, Dr West's secretary, knew me from my meetings with him. She was apologetic, saying she was sorry I had to find out about his passing that way.

I got my thoughts together and told her why I had called. That I needed another medical report for Kevin's case to try and take it through Europe. Sue gave me the name of the man who had taken Dr West's place at Guy's, Dr Nathaniel Carey. I was grateful to her for that.

I contacted Dr Carey and explained my situation. He said he had no problem doing a report for me because Dr West had left all his files and personal notes on Kevin so I said I would arrange a date to travel to London to see him. I managed to set up a meeting with Ed as well.

Another thing that I had been doing, not long beforehand, paid off. I had spent a lot of time writing to all kinds of different people asking for help and publicity, explaining what had happened to Kevin at Hillsborough and what we were trying to achieve. One of those people to write back to me was Sir Richard Branson.

Sir Richard wrote me some lovely letters over the years and showed what a generous man he is. He offered us free train travel whenever we needed to see our legal or medical teams. He gave me a contact number for Elsa Redpath, who was in charge of Virgin Trains, and all I had to do was to ring her when we needed tickets. To my surprise we were allocated first class tickets every time we travelled. It was a fantastic gesture from Sir Richard.

When Sheila and I met up at Lime Street Station to get the train to London to see Dr Carey and Ed, I spotted John Barnes. He was getting on the same carriage as us.

I had met John once before and I wanted to speak to him. He was one of Kevin's heroes.

I decided to wait until we had had our breakfast. Then, John got up to go to the gents. To do so he had to pass our table. This was my chance.

"Hiya," I said to him as he walked past. He stopped, looked at me and straight away he said, "I know you. Where from?"

I told him I was one of the Hillsborough families and we were going to see our barrister to see if we had a case for Europe.

"Go for it," he replied. "Get the bastards." And then he gave me a kiss!

John was one of Kevin's favourite players and had

been on the pitch at Hillsborough, in the Liverpool team, before the game was abandoned. I felt that seeing him on the train was a good omen, but I was still nervous about how the meetings would go.

Dr Carey was very nice and just as helpful as Dr West had always been. That was a relief. Ed Fitzgerald, as usual, was very pleased to see me and Sheila and offered to help in any way he could.

We went over the evidence and Ed explained that Kevin's case did relate to Section 2 of the Human Rights Act. Ed told us he would do the draft with the new evidence I had found since the last submission. We were back fighting the system.

The train journey home was a happy one – even without John Barnes sat near to us. We had enough evidence to go into Europe and back to the Attorney General. It felt like a couple of doors had opened. That we were getting somewhere.

I kept in touch with Dr Carey's secretary, who was also his wife, and the next time we arranged a meeting with him, Sheila and I were invited to attend a memorial service in remembrance of Dr West in the chapel at Guy's Hospital.

Dr Carey had arranged to meet us at Euston Station on the same day and we used a quiet room in the Virgin Lounge there to meet. I gave him the evidence and he said he would send for the autopsy photos and do a report for me. We then made our way to Guys for Dr

Iain West's service.

The chapel was lovely and a lot of pathologists spoke very highly of Dr West. Afterwards, Dr Carey came over to us with a lovely lady and introduced her as Vesna West, Iain's wife.

She thanked me for all the letters I had written to Dr West over the years and invited Sheila and I to the memorial dinner. That was very nice of her.

Everything was in place for the Attorney General, now. This time around it was Peter Goldsmith, who was actually from Liverpool. I hoped that might give us a better chance as he might know how strong feelings were about the cover-up, but it was the same old story. "Not in the interests of justice," was his verdict. Knocked back again. So much for third time lucky.

Ed Fitzgerald said to me again afterwards, "If Kevin had not died at Hillsborough, Anne, you would have got your inquest a long time ago."

We all knew why they wouldn't give it to me. It would open a big can of worms over just how much corruption had gone on to hide the truth. But I was still wasn't going to give up.

As planned, I submitted to Europe and then just had to wait. I felt this was the best way to go, but there were some differences of opinion within the Hillsborough Justice Campaign. I thought about it carefully and came to the conclusion that I had to leave the group. To go it alone.

The HJC wished me well with Europe and I must say that I am thankful for the many wonderful people I met because of my involvement with them.

They have helped many families and counselled so many survivors. They provide a wonderful support network for people who still have to live with the effects of Hillsborough and probably will always have to.

Some survivors buried what happened to them and just tried to block it out, but as time has gone by it has, inevitably, caught up with them. How could it not?

This is where the HJC is so important. It gives them a place to go to help each other and you simply cannot put a price on having that support.'

Even at this stage of things, over 15 years after the disaster, Mum was still meeting survivors who were only just coming to terms with what they had gone through.

For a long time she thought she had found out as much about Kevin's last hour as she was ever going to, but she was wrong. Another lifelong Liverpool supporter, John Herbert, came forward.

John had been in Pen 3 of the Leppings Lane end, caught up in the crush like Kev was, and had been struggling to deal with what he went through.

A friend of his called John Miller, who knew he had been at Hillsborough and was following Mum's case, bought her book for him, knowing he would be interested in the story. He couldn't believe what he saw.

John's story...

'As soon as I pulled Anne's book out of the bag, I nearly fell over. I recognised Kevin's face instantly from the photo on the cover.

I knew that he was the kid who I'd tried to help in the middle of the crush and who had been haunting my dreams ever since.

I had been in Pen 3 with my mate Kenny and Kev was carried across us in one of the surges as the crush developed.

He was on his knees, so I grabbed him by the shoulder and tried to drag him up, but it was impossible. I couldn't move one hand at that point, but my other one was holding my bobble hat and my ticket so I let them go and got hold of him.

To pull someone up you need to be able to bend your arm, but there wasn't the room to do so. Kev was getting dragged down and slipping sideways, but I had a good grip on him for a while.

Kenny was also getting sucked down into it, but I grabbed him by the back of the jeans and we were sort of leaning forward at this crazy angle, getting swirled about.

This went on for a good few minutes and I remember an ambulance pulling up in front of the terrace and a Liverpool scarf being thrown across the windscreen.

Then the crush barrier collapsed.

We all fell over. I lost hold of Kevin and that was the last I saw of him.

I always thought 'he's gone', because of where he was. Where me and Kenny were, it was only our legs that were trapped so our upper bodies were out of it. But we couldn't move.

We were lying on a pile of bodies and the pain in my legs was so bad that I thought they were snapped all the way up. I kept saying "sorry" to the fella in front of me, "it's not me."

Somehow we got pulled up a bit, but still couldn't really move. I looked at Kenny. He'd passed out before and seemed to be in trouble again.

He said to me, "John, I'm going." At first I joked to him, "Take me with you." But he was about to get married and they'd just had a baby so I got angry with him.

I said to him, "What, so I've got to go home and tell your missus? I've got to see her and say, 'I tried, love, but you know, sorry?'"

So I butted him and bit his ear to keep him awake. He always moans now that I broke his cheekbone and gave him the worst wedgie of his life, but I did what I had to do.

Gradually there was a bit more room and we managed to get ourselves up. Somehow we were alright.

Kenny was still a bit wobbly, but I was fine, even though earlier I'd thought my legs were broken.

There was a kind of well of bodies at the foot of the terrace and I started dragging people out, as many as I could.

I remember one lad who had this jumper on with a houndstooth pattern who we were trying to drag out of it up towards the back of the terrace. I was banging on his chest to try and wake him up. But then a police officer appeared from somewhere and pushed me off.

I just sat there on the terrace with this pile of bodies in front of me.

I stopped going the match after that. And I kept it all in, really. There didn't seem to be anywhere for survivors to go and talk about things.

I couldn't really talk about it with my mum and dad as I didn't want to upset them and there was the macho thing where even the lads I went to Hillsborough with wouldn't talk about it.

When the McGovern documentary was on I rang one of the helplines the next day, but I didn't exactly get the best reception. Their attitude seemed to be 'well, it's a bit late now'.

I didn't really know much about exactly what had happened at Hillsborough until that point, just my own experience and what some of the other lads had said on the way home.

So, seeing Kevin on the front of the book brought it all back for me. He'd been on my mind constantly. I'd had nightmares about him, but I didn't really feel I could tell anyone at that time. I started to think about contacting Anne, but didn't know how to. What would I even say to her? Where do you start?

On the 14th anniversary, in 2003, I was leaving Anfield after the memorial service and as I walked past The Albert pub I saw Anne stood outside talking to people.

I thought to myself, 'Now's your chance, go and talk to her'. But I just couldn't do it.

It was years later when I did finally get in touch.

I asked a lot of my girl friends who are mums how they would feel if they were Anne. Would they want to know? I took their responses on board and I ended up joining Anne's 'Hope For Hillsborough' Facebook group.

I still didn't know what to do, though, and beat myself up about it a bit. But then, one night, I bit the bullet. I sent her a message.

We arranged to meet and she came to my house with her friend, George Tomkins. We had a cup of tea and a chat and then she said, "Ok then, tell me."

I was pretty scared of the reaction I might get when I told her what had happened. I thought she'd want to kill me, but it was completely the other end of the spectrum. Anne was brilliant.

She totally put me at ease and told me it wasn't my fault. She couldn't have been more supportive.

She said to me it felt like she found the different elements of Kevin's story backwards, but I was able to put a piece of it into place that she didn't have before. She was happy with that.

People used to ask me how I was so sure it was Kevin that I was with on the Leppings Lane. But I remembered his face and his hair as much as anything.

Even so, when I met Anne that first time I said to her "I'm not going to just tell you it was your kid. I'll tell what I saw – what I remember – and we'll take it from there."

I described his jumper. His hair. And, with an apology, his sticky-out ears. Straight away, Anne said it was Kevin that I had described.

Anne saved my soul, really, because I was in a mess. I wasn't sleeping or eating properly, but we became mates and she helped me with a lot of the things about Hillsborough that I hadn't ever dealt with.

I'd go up to Chester to see her for a weekend or she'd come to me and we'd just spend time together. Go for a drink, watch a film or often end up gabbing until all hours.

We always used to look out for each other and make sure we were eating and sleeping ok. She'd tell me off, and vice versa, if I wasn't looking after myself properly.

A group of us would sometimes go to Anfield on a matchday, not to go to the game, but just to watch it in The Sandon with a few drinks and meet up with people.

Anne joined us for one game, Liverpool against Arsenal, on the opening day of a season.

We were sitting there in the pub and she said she was starving, so we went to one of those vans by the ground to get something to eat. She decided she wanted a hot dog but when they gave it to her it was massive, about a foot long. She looked quite shocked, told me I'd have to have half of it and then goes to the poor harassed girl behind the counter, "Eh love, can you cut this in half for us?"

She didn't really want to, but Anne kept on at her, "Just chop it in half. You've got a knife there, haven't you?" The girl did in the end and we just sat there on this little wall in front of someone's house munching on half a giant hot dog each.

But that was Anne. I've never met a more determined woman.

The way she fought and fought against every obstacle put in her way – it's a mother's love thing, for me. If a mother knows she's right then nothing can stop her.'

John Herbert

Another survivor's story that Mum was particularly interested in was that of Dean Harris. Dean is a police officer now, but in 1989 he was a 16-year-old Liverpool supporter who was in Pen 4 at the Leppings Lane end.

That Dean was 16, just a year older than Kev, struck

a chord with Mum. He described her as "the mum of Hillsborough" because she played a big part in educating him, and quite a few other survivors, on what had happened to them on that fateful day. Her empathy, sympathy and understanding of what they'd been through endeared her to Dean.

Mum wanted people to know about Kevin's case, but she was interested in everybody else's story as well. She opened her arms out to everyone.

Dean has said that it makes him proud to see the banners on the Kop dedicated to Mum and feel the affection that flows towards her from all around the world.

The fight for justice became ingrained in her through her own hard work. She found all the missing pieces of the jigsaw puzzle of Kev's story and was not going to give it up, no matter how many times the system closed ranks against her, until her mission was complete.

"I don't think there are too many people that could have carried on like Anne did," says Dean, "but she never lost that capacity to open her heart to other people.

"I was 16 at the time, just a year older than Kevin. I was in Pen 4, but directly adjacent to where he was in Pen 3, on the opposite side of the fence.

"For whatever reason I went left instead of right when I got in the ground. Fate, I suppose. That choice may well have saved my life.

"Anne wanted to know all about my experiences that

day. It must have been painful for her to hear, but she was so determined to build up an accurate picture of what actually happened.

"I felt guilty about telling her certain things, like ringing home that day to tell my folks I was ok. I know that call is what she was waiting for from Kevin, what she was praying for, but never received. She was pleased to hear my story, though, and always tried to put my mind at ease. She became my 'Hillsborough mum'.

"I often feel there are strong parallels between myself and Kevin and I think Anne did too, which is probably why we became so close. She met my mum and dad when I brought them up to the memorial service one year and she would always ask after them."

There were, and still are, many survivors still struggling after what happened to them at Hillsborough, but Mum just took them under her wing.

When Facebook really took off it provided the perfect vehicle for her to keep in touch with a lot of survivors, particularly those like Dean who live far away and are quite isolated from any support.

If ever anything hurtful about Hillsborough came out in the news, which of course would bring things flooding back for everyone involved, Mum's Facebook page would become the focal point for people to go to and make sure that everyone was ok. I know it became an absolutely invaluable support system for many of them.

They were able to get into conversations on there and

look out for each other. For some there was nowhere else to turn to, but a bond has been formed between people from all kinds of different backgrounds that will never be broken.

"Anne was like a mother figure to us all on there," adds Dean. "She often used to start her updates with 'Good evening, My Red Family' and that really is what it felt like. She would stick up for us whenever something bad came out as if we were her own children.

"It felt incredible that she would be the one asking if we were ok when she must have been so upset at the things that were happening herself, but she was so strong and she passed that fortitude onto us. She was always thinking of how other people would be affected by what was happening, which says everything about her.

"I was so honoured when she would ask me to support her at various meetings or events that were happening.

"She built a group around herself of people from all different backgrounds and walks of life. I'm a police officer, Tony O'Keefe is a firefighter – there are people from everywhere who feel that, because of the support she gave us, we would have followed her to the end of the earth in her mission to right the wrongs of Hillsborough if need be.

"And she knows we'll see it through for her."

One of those people who is playing his part in 'seeing

it through' for Mum is Ian Barnes, one of Kev's school friends. He'd met Mum a few times when he was a kid, coming to parties at our house and later at a couple of events at Formby High after Hillsborough.

He subsequently moved to Liverpool and hadn't seen Mum for years, but had always followed her fight for the truth when it was in the news and often wondered how she was getting on.

He saw a post on a Liverpool supporters forum saying that she was now operating on her own and wondered whether she might need some help so asked the lad who had posted the message on the forum to pass his number on to her. Mum soon got in touch.

They met up and, having left the HJC, Mum told Ian how she was thinking of setting up her own group. He'd never been involved in anything like that before, but had some organisational experience through his work as a trade union rep.

Ian told her that he would look after all the admin side of things for her so she could just concentrate on the campaign and, after a few more meetings, Mum came up with the idea of 'Hope For Hillsborough' as the name of her new group in the summer of 2008.

The first fundraiser they organised was a race night. They started putting the word around on things like MySpace, Friends Reunited and Facebook, although Ian tells me they didn't understand properly how those websites worked at that point!

They knew they needed to raise their profile, though, and managed to get something in the Liverpool Echo. The night went really well, making nearly £5,000 and further fundraising events followed. They had t-shirts done as well. Mum had one she liked with the names of all the victims arranged as a big 96, so Ian slightly tweaked that with the help of some design students at Liverpool University. They got them made so people could buy them to support the campaign.

Kevin Reavey, from the Poor Scouser Tommy web-site, came forward as well and they paid to have the logo made into a massive banner, which has been taken to Liverpool games ever since. They even got it copy-right protected. It always gave Mum a lift when she saw a clip of that banner on TV during the match or a picture of it in the paper. It helped keep Hillsborough in people's minds, which is what she was trying to do.

Of course it was very frustrating for Mum to still be waiting for a response from Europe, but it helped her to know that people still cared. If there's one thing the people of Merseyside have always been known for, it's how to stick together.

Also in 2008, the country's first ever football support-ers union was launched by a group of Reds unhappy with, amongst other things, the effect Tom Hicks and George Gillett's ownership was beginning to have on Liverpool Football Club. They called themselves Spirit of Shankly.

Fran Stanton was one of the founding committee members and, after a chance meeting on the Kop at Anfield, the SOS went on to become great supporters of Mum.

"I remember exactly when I first met Anne," Fran recalls. "It was the 19th anniversary of Hillsborough and as I walked down the steps at the front of the Kop following the memorial service, I bumped into Peter Carney, a lifelong Red who I had known for some time through his community work in the city and the re-cently created Spirit of Shankly Liverpool supporters union.

"Peter introduced us. I knew who Anne was because of the story of Kevin and her battle since, but we had never met. A few thoughts crossed my mind on that first occasion. One was 'why is Anne sat by Peter and his friend and not in the official family seats?'

"My other thought, literally within the first thirty sec-onds, was how gentle and unassuming her manner was – little did I know! – a bit like the scene in Braveheart where Mel Gibson says he couldn't possibly be Wil-liam Wallace because he isn't 8ft tall and isn't shooting lightning bolts from his arse.

"I guess I just didn't know what to expect from some-one who had battled the establishment for the last 19 years in the name of her son to look like. Anne just reminded me of a normal down to earth woman. A mum."

Afterwards, Mum went to The Albert next to the ground where she, Fran, Peter and George Tomkins sat and discussed the stories and topics that generally get discussed following the memorial service every year.

Mum spoke about her repeated attempts to get the Attorney General to use the compelling evidence she had amounted and tracked down over the years to re-open an inquest into Kevin's death. How she had been continually refused.

She was certain and so determined that the evidence she had possessed for many years already, which would eventually come out to such fanfare from the Hillsborough Independent Panel four years later, would be enough to have inquests into all the deaths re-opened.

This was the first time Fran had heard of such information and they began to discuss how Spirit of Shankly could possibly help Mum publicise her campaign and fight for justice.

They agreed to meet later that week to speak about how they could promote the campaign and around the same time the Spirit of Shankly management committee met.

SOS agreed that they would not take the lead on any campaigning around Hillsborough, or the fight for justice, as there were already well established groups who were more knowledgeable and experienced on the subject.

What was agreed was that SOS would help any of

these groups in any way possible with any support they may need with the particular campaigns.

Fran arranged to meet Anne later in the week and when she got to the Black Horse pub in Walton it looked as though the back part of the pub had been turned into an office.

Anne, Peter and George were sat at a table covered in folders, dossiers and boxes of paperwork.

"I sat down and Anne began to speak about some of the evidence she had in her possession," Fran explains, "including evidence from WPC Debra Martin stating it was around 4pm on the day when Kevin passed away, which of course is why Anne and so many others were unhappy about the 3.15pm cut-off point.

"George then began to speak about not only the disaster, but the cover up that followed, particularly regarding the 'investigation' into the behaviour of South Yorkshire Police by West Midlands Police force and the role of Detective Superintendent Stanley Beechey.

"It was completely shocking to hear how George had been treated by this individual and I was glad for him that he had been able to win his court case against the West Midlands Police. To find out Beechey had been so strongly involved in Hillsborough, to the extent of being tasked with presenting the audio tapes of David Duckenfield and other officers for the inquests in court, was just unbelievable.

"I always knew what had happened at Hillsborough

was very wrong, but this was probably the first time I realised just how disgusting the cover-up had been.

"I also felt a bit embarrassed that these people felt the need to try and win me and SOS around with the evidence. I made a point of saying they had nothing to prove to me and we would do whatever we could to help in any way we could.

"Anne said that she was just so used to hitting brick walls and feeling like she was doing this on her own that this was the only real way of winning people over, using the cold, hard evidence.

"We got to work. I posted on some LFC forums, using the kudos I had gained from being in SOS to speak about Anne's plight, the evidence she had, her attempts to go back to the Attorney General and the European High Court. It raised a fire and anger with the group of lads I went the match with and other friends.

"Why is Anne on her own? Why isn't all this evidence being seen? What can we do?

"I had known Ian Barnes for a while through mutual friends and we worked together to throw the SOS's backing behind whatever fundraisers Hope For Hillsborough were doing.

"It was during this period that I really became aware of the split in the campaign groups, fractures that looked like they were healing following the release of the HIP report. But back in 2008 I was getting phone calls from well known Reds, people I had respected for a long time, questioning me. 'What's all the money being used for? You know what she is doing with it all, don't you?'

"Our response to this was we didn't give two fucks what the money was going to be used for. After searching for evidence, tracking down police officers and campaigning for her dead son for 19 years, if Anne wanted to book herself on a cruise around the world for 12 months, not one of us would have batted an eyelid. It would be the least she deserved.

"But even letting these thoughts cross our mind shows we had no way of measuring just how tenacious and determined Anne was in her crusade to get justice for Kevin, and all those who died at Hillsborough.

"That very first event, a race night at the Silvestrian Club near Scotland Road and attended by about 350 people, will always live in the memory of those who were there. Peter Carney had dressed the room so it looked like an Aladdin's cave of LFC and everyone had a brilliant time.

"At the end of the evening a teary-eyed Anne got on the mic to speak and the room hushed.

"She spoke about how she had walked through a storm and a lot of the time felt like she was doing it on her own, but nights like this, and the people in attendance, had shown her that she did have support and wasn't doing this alone.

"Grown men openly cried at her words. Anne Williams, this 5ft 5in mother from Merseyside, had turned into their leader."

Mum's speech moved on to the fight for justice, the battle against the government and how the evidence she had put together meant it was only a matter of time before everyone knew the real truth about Hillsborough. From that night on, the people in the room would have ran through a brick wall for her.

And what did she do with the money raised? Book a cruise? As if! Mum used it to set up a recognised charity, 'For Justice', to work alongside the Hope For Hillsborough campaign group.

More interest poured in. Mum couldn't believe it at first. There were other events like a '70s/'80s night and the lads from the Irish Kop website put on a race night over in Ireland soon afterwards.

Then she went international! It was all thanks to a Liverpool fan called Jason Morland and a few of his mates, none of whom she'd ever even met before. They just wanted to help. People are lovely sometimes.

Jason and his friend Phil Belger had got to know a Norwegian lad called Olav Rosvold through going to the match and we'd been friends for years.

Olav would come to stay with Jason when he was over and has put the lads up when they've gone over there. He suggested that they should have a charity match – Scouse Reds v Norwegian Wools, they decided to call it – with the funds going to a Hillsborough appeal.

None of them actually knew Mum at the time, but they were all aware of what she was trying to do and decided to support her. They felt that because she seemed to be on her own, as opposed to the other groups who obviously had more people in them, she deserved some support.

"We got in touch with her through Fran Stanton and the Spirit of Shankly, and we were absolutely made up when Anne was able to attend on the day," said Jason. "She turned up with a friend and watched from the dug-out before presenting the trophies at the end.

"I remember us talking beforehand saying how we didn't want the match to be too one-sided as for some stupid reason we honestly thought we were going to win about 10-0!

"It was a completely different story on the day as we soon found the Norwegian Wools were very handy indeed. They even had a couple of ex-professionals in their team.

"We had decided before the game to go for 30 minutes each way rather than 45 and it was a good job as they came flying out of the traps and went one nil up in the first half with a goal from Stein Thorkidsen.

"It wasn't until late on in the second half that they seemed to tire and we suddenly got three quick goals from Carlos Navarro, Jacko and Carl Hibbard. Olav still reckons the referee was biased and played 45 minutes of 'Fergie time' in the second half, but I'm not having that.

"We had arranged a do afterwards at the Village Inn nearby and the landlady, Libby Orr, did us proud. When we turned up, they had put red and white bunting all over the outside of the pub. They laid food on for us and the lads had hung up loads of Liverpool flags and Hillsborough justice banners all over the place which really brightened everything up and made it feel like a special occasion.

"We got a really fantastic turn-out. It is quite a big pub, but it was packed in there because so many people had turned up.

"Anne brought a box load of her books and t-shirts and sold out of them all in no time.

"We had a Jam tribute band on and over the course of the evening we managed to raise £4,500 for Anne's charity which we were all absolutely made up with.

"There was a raffle and auctions of signed kits, balls and other bits of memorabilia and prizes. My mate Phil, who had helped me organise everything, was the auctioneer.

"We auctioned off a signed Fernando Torres Spain top and the bids went up very quickly in multiples of £10. It was his first season at Liverpool and he was on fire at the time, everybody loved him.

"It turned into a three-way battle between Olav Rosvold, Carlos Navarro and Ste McCarthy. Carlos had to back out at £250. He was gutted as he'd set his heart on the top. It then continued up to £550 where it looked like Ste had pulled out as well, but just before Phil said "sold," Ste come back in with £560 so on it went. The atmosphere was a mixture of tension and laughter after each bid. It carried on until Ste eventually won. With a bid of £950!"

During all this, Mum had sat open-mouthed. Jason recalls seeing her mouthing the words, "I can't believe it." Her head was swivelling back and forth like she was watching a tennis match between the two bidders. She went and gave Steve a big hug at the end.

It turned into a night that I think they'll always remember, but I wish someone had recorded the speech she made. Jason describes it as an amazing, emotional and inspirational moment.

"It was unbelievable as the packed pub fell silent to listen to her," continues Jason. "She had no doubt she would win in the end and the truth would come out.

"The thing which always stuck out to me and my mates, though, was that she repeatedly said during her speech, 'You survivors are just as much victims of Hillsborough as me.'

"I couldn't believe that someone who had lost her beloved son could say this, but you could see she genuinely meant it. It'll stick with me forever.

"I've got two kids myself and can only imagine how I would have coped with what she went through.

"She was so passionate about what she was doing.

You knew when she said 'we will get the truth, justice will be done,' that she absolutely meant it.

"I had my doubts as to whether there would ever be any real breakthrough on Hillsborough, but she was just adamant there would be one day. She had total belief.

"And she was right."

12

Breaking Through

'She dabbed a tear from her eye and said,
'How could they not see what was going on?'

STILL Mum waited for an answer from Europe. It had been more than two years now and the twentieth anniversary was drawing near. The wait was agonising.

Real Radio, who were always very supportive of Mum and what she was trying to do, wanted to make a documentary where they would take her to Hillsborough as part of their coverage.

She'd never actually been to the ground and I don't think she really wanted to go on her own.

Finlay wasn't even six months old, so I couldn't go, so Mum asked Stevie Hart to go with her. It was something he had to think through, having never been back there himself since 1989.

"I'd never ever have considered going back to Hillsborough, but for Anne," admits Stevie. "As was often the way though, she'd ring me up and go, 'Ste, I've set up an interview with x and y, you don't mind speaking to them do you? No, of course you don't.'

"I didn't, normally, but this time I thought to myself, 'I really don't fancy that'.

"What I didn't realise, though, was that Anne had never been to Hillsborough. She'd never set foot inside the ground in which Kevin had died.

"I always assumed she had, but when I discovered that she hadn't I felt that I couldn't let her down over something like this. I agreed to go."

Mum had worked with the guy involved from Real Radio, Christian Spooner, before and knew he was someone she could trust. He drove them both there, all the way over the Pennines on a freezing cold winter's day, to the scene of British football's worse sporting disaster. A place that had changed all of our lives irrevocably.

Real Radio had managed to gain permission to go inside the ground.

Stevie continues: "We went in the stand to the right of the Leppings Lane, the same side as the dug-outs, and the first thing you see is the police control box and the tunnels, both in exactly the same places as they were previously. I don't know why I assumed they'd be somewhere different, but I did.

"Within minutes everything came flooding back. In 1988 I'd gone with my dad and we'd actually been directed to the side pens. He died in February '89.

"We sat down in that side stand for a bit. Everything was flashing by as we were doing the interview. I was pointing things out, 'this is where we picked him up, this is where we set him down and so on.'

"Anne was looking around everywhere, taking everything in, and then Christian took us down into the Leppings Lane end itself.

"I just pointed out things like where I was standing, where the gate was. Then they wanted to walk down the tunnel, but there was no way I could do that, even with Anne.

"So we went outside and I showed him the turnstile where I went in and the gate that was opened, but there was no way I could walk down there again.

"Anne did, though, and she was pleased that she had gone and been able to get through it."

It says everything about Stevie that he was able to put himself through an ordeal like that for Mum.

He said afterwards he had hated every minute of it, but it helped her piece everything together in her mind and visualise things.

It also helped that Christian was very understanding and sensitive about what the experience might be like for them both and didn't make it any more difficult for them than it needed to be.

He was great with Mum and she was always happy to do anything with Real Radio as they became big supporters of what she was trying to do at a time when not many other media companies were interested.

"From the minute I first met Anne, three things shone through – determination, anger, and love," says Christian.

"Anger at the authorities for the injustice she had been forced to endure for so many years. Determination that she would eventually get justice for her son. And an overwhelming sense of love every time she smiled while mentioning 'our Kev'.

"When I first went to Anne's house to discuss making a radio documentary, I never set out to form a friendship. It just sort of happened. We immediately got on and it was impossible not to respect her dignity and courage.

"I feel honoured that she clearly had faith in me and trusted me enough to take her on such a difficult journey – her first visit to Hillsborough.

"Truthfully, I never set out to make that journey with her. When I asked Anne if she'd ever been inside the stadium, I expected her to say yes, a number of times. When she said no, I asked her if she would like to go.

"I fully expected her to react angrily saying that she could never contemplate setting foot in that ground –

and who would have blamed her? But when she slowly looked up at me and quietly replied 'I wouldn't mind,' I set about trying to make it happen.

"It was a bitterly cold February morning when I drove Anne and Stevie over to Sheffield. Anne had only asked Stevie to come along the night before we were due to make the journey.

"As we wound our way over the snowy Pennines, the enormity of what we were doing really hit me. While Anne was chatting away, clutching a bunch of flowers which she'd brought to lay at the memorial, I looked in the rear view mirror at Stevie who was sitting in near silence.

"It truly struck me for the first time that this was probably going to be harder for Stevie than it would be for Anne. Yes, I was taking Anne to see, for the first time, the spot where Kevin had been fatally injured... but Stevie hadn't been to Hillsborough since April 15, 1989.

"He had survived Leppings Lane, heroically ferrying injured supporters across the pitch on advertising boards – and would no doubt have flashbacks on this trip. It's a measure of the man that he put his fears to one side, feeling duty bound to go back with Anne so that he could show her where things had unfolded and where Kevin had been.

"I can clearly remember us walking up the steps in the South Stand and seeing the rows of blue seats melting into view. At the top, we stopped and turned left to look over at Leppings Lane. Stevie was visibly shaking – unable to believe that the tunnel still existed. Anne's disbelief and anger were palpable. Having only ever seen TV footage, she was shocked that the ground appeared so much smaller than on video.

"As we walked slowly over to Leppings Lane and towards the police control box, she dabbed a tear from her eye with a tissue, turned to me and repeatedly said 'how could they not have seen what was going on?'

"We spent most of an hour inside the stadium. It was clear Anne was trying to work out Kevin's last movements and where he would have been. Her years of research instinctively told her not to walk on a certain area of concrete – she told me she knew that's where a number of bodies had been.

"Light snow began falling as Anne and I walked through the dank, dark tunnel to look at where Gate C had been and where Kevin would have walked. She wanted to see everything. She wanted to re-trace Kevin's steps.

"Before we started making our way back to the car to get some food, Anne told me that she could 'feel the fight coming back' and that 'maybe Kev's spirit's here.'

She ended the documentary by insisting that she would get justice. She vowed that she would never go away.

"And, true to her word, Anne continued to fight –

eventually seeing the truth emerge in the Hillsborough Independent Panel report – and crucially seeing Kevin's accidental death verdict quashed."

Going back to Hillsborough felt like putting another one of the building blocks in place for Mum.

She was so thorough about all her work on Hillsborough there was very little that was new she could have found out, but she just felt it was something she needed to do. I found her own memories of that trip on her computer. This is what Mum wrote:

'I just could not believe how small the ground was. It looked so much bigger on the videos that I had seen.

We just stood in the stand and then Stevie pointed to a hoarding across the other side of the pitch. "That's where we put Kevin down," he said. I did not realise Kevin had been so close to the corner where the ambulances should have been coming in.

We walked in silence to the Leppings Lane end. The control box was right over the pens and they had all the zoom-in cameras so they would have been able to see right into them.

The zoom on the cameras was good enough to be able to see the colour of people's eyes, apparently. How the police could not see how full Pens 3 and 4 were will always baffle me.

We started to walk along the gap between the small wall where the perimeter fencing would have been.

Stevie was upset and was talking to Christian so I carried on walking. I then realised If I carried on I would have walked on that part of the ground where everyone would have fallen down when the barrier had broken. I moved back onto the pitch. It was eerie. I did not want to walk on that area. It felt like I would be walking over a mass grave.

I could see poor Stevie was still struggling, but I had to keep going. I stood back to count the seats that would have been Pen 3. 420 seats yet they had herded over 2,000 people into that small area. Unbelievable.

I was really upset by this point myself. It was cold and had started to snow. All those poor people who had died in the most dreadful circumstances. Right where I was stood. I looked up the steps and saw the entrance to the tunnel. I wanted to go through and see Gate C. Christian and Stevie joined me on the pitch but, understandably, Stevie could not go near the tunnel. He stayed back and I just went with Christian.

It was ok until I got half way and realised people had died in there. It was a terrible feeling. I could not wait to get out. Once I did, I was surprised again at how small the area was between Gate C and the tunnel. It looked a much bigger area on the videos. I could see now how, once they had been let in, the fans who had been fighting for their lives outside the ground would have gone straight to the tunnel thinking it would lead to all the terraces and not just pens 3 and 4.

We made our way back through the tunnel to find Stevie. It was getting really cold so we decided to make our way to the Hillsborough memorial, which is situated outside the stadium, to lay our flowers for the 96.

Walking back to the car we went down lots of little streets. Stevie was saying how all the front doors had been open on the day and the people of Sheffield were letting the Liverpool fans use their telephones to ring home. That was kind of them. A gesture that shouldn't be forgotten.

I did not regret going to Hillsborough, but I was very shocked about the size of the ground and the position of the police control box...'

Finally, Europe came back with an answer to Mum, two weeks before the 20th anniversary. They may as well not have bothered. Mum could not have a new inquest into Kevin's death because she was "out of time".

The ruling said that because the European Court regarded the Stuart-Smith stitch-up in 1997 as being the last legal process in this country, the application should have been submitted within six months of that.

What a joke. How can justice have a best-before date?

I was furious. If they'd have said at the start about this time issue then at least Mum would have been aware of it and wouldn't have wasted more than two years waiting for them to get off their backsides and tell her what they knew all along.

I used to think a lot about those words Europe knocked her back with. 'Out of time'. They seem to take on even more meaning now.

A lad from the Red and White Kop website, Mark Ballard, wrote a lovely poem afterwards which was forwarded onto Mum via Spirit of Shankly.

It gave her a bit of a lift.

Out of sight,
Out of mind.
What can we tell her?
'Out of time'.

But Kevin Williams was out of time,
Fifteen years old – the authorities' crime.
And time the inquiries chose to block,
Between 3:15 and four o'clock.

Those minutes when Kevin was still here,
Those minutes the authorities have come to fear,
Those minutes omitted from the party line,
Were they even counted in 'out of time?'

Those minutes that ambulances sat outside,
When violence inside was implied,
When fans saved lives and police stood in line,
Do those minutes count towards 'out of time?'

Sara Williams

What about the hours when police covered up,
Questions of drinking and 'were they late turning up?'
Questions when their children had just lost their lives,
Do these hours count in your 'out of time?'

Did you count the days when the myths were passed on,
While families were mourning their daughters and sons,
The time that the press spent telling their lies,
Did you count those days when saying 'you're out of time?'

And what about the years this woman has fought,
The years many families have been distraught,
The years of tears we all have cried,
Do those years count towards 'out of time?'

Out of sight,
But in our minds.
Keep fighting Anne,
We're by your side.

Mum was as philosophical as ever. "I'm used to the setbacks now anyway," she said to me. "And it's not like they've refused me because they've said I'm wrong. It's because of this timing thing. So we'll try something else."

Stevie was still well up for the fight as well.

"It was a blow because we were convinced that Europe would be our biggest and best chance," he says.

198

"This was the one that would make the breakthrough and blow the whole thing wide open. There was never any mention of a time constraint when we applied.

"The right to life was something that they brought out themselves! You kind of expect to get shafted in this country, but the whole idea of the European Court of Human Rights always struck a chord with me, just the name of it made me think of it as a place where justice at least had a chance of flourishing. Turns out they were just words.

"But, as usual, Anne wasn't throwing in the towel. And, frustrating though it was, she was right in that it wasn't like they'd told her 'you don't have a case'. It had been refused on a technicality. They actually said we should submit again to the Attorney General. In other words 'Don't give up, but we're not helping you!'

"So it was a setback, but at the same time it did encourage us to keep going although we knew that the next crack at the Attorney General would be very much the last chance saloon."

We were still getting our heads around the knock-back from Europe and suddenly it was the 20th anniversary. April 15 is a day you just try and steel yourself to get through, but we knew this year would feel a bit different. I suppose a landmark number like '20' is always going to feel that bit more significant.

Little did we know just how much of an impact it would turn out to have.

I just couldn't believe it had been twenty years. Sometimes it only felt like yesterday. We were expecting a
good turn-out for the service at Anfield. Mum and me
still went every year although we'd stopped going into
the complex before it started, where you would get a
cup of tea and meet up with other families, after the
tenth anniversary.

Sheffield Wednesday Football Club had finally decided to give us a memorial stone at the ground in
1999, after persistent pressure from the HJC, and the
anniversary fell only a couple of weeks before the proposed boycott of Liverpool's Premier League match at
Hillsborough.

The idea of a boycott had been in people's minds for
a while. In May 1997, the day after the Justice concert at Anfield, fans – including bereaved families and
survivors – had flowers and banners confiscated from
them before the Reds' game there. The same thing
happened again the following season, with that match
also being sponsored, just for good measure, by The
Sun newspaper. Enough was enough.

Again, Liverpool were due to play there in the May
and there was plenty of support for a no-show. Barnes
Travel, a local travel firm who have run coach trips to
Liverpool and Everton away games for years, refused to
take bookings as a mark of respect for the families and
survivors, and a concert attended by over 5,000 people
was organised for St George's Hall, which ended up

being a roaring success. Only about 1,000 out of the 7,500 seats in the Leppings Lane end were taken up that day, although conveniently enough Liverpool's first game of the following season, which people are always desperate to go to, was Sheffield Wednesday away in order to guarantee them a good crowd. I thought that was pathetic.

So feelings were running even higher than usual before that tenth anniversary. We were having a cup of tea in the complex beforehand, chatting with Dr Ed Walker.

He had been one of the first doctors in attendance at the Northern General Hospital in Sheffield on the day and his statements, confirming that he had tried to save fans who sadly later died but were alive well after 3.15pm, had gone 'missing' for nine years. He had been a big help to Mum and it was nice of him to come all that way to pay his respects on the anniversary.

We were gabbing away when I noticed that there seemed to be quite a few police there. High-ranking ones as well with pips on their shoulders. I didn't understand who they were or why they were there.

When Dr Walker told us it was the chief constable of South Yorkshire Police, who had actually been invited to attend, we could not believe it. We were so upset that we never went in the complex before the service again.

You do understand as you get older that not all coppers are bad, but I speak to survivors and can understand how the attitude you get from some police when you've been stopped for speeding or something can bring a lot of things flooding back for them. It was Mum who convinced me that there are plenty who try and do the right thing, but it took a while!

From then on, anyway, we would always meet up with some other families and the survivors who gather by the HJC shop and march around the ground with banners and flowers to lay at the memorial on Anfield Road.

Even outside the ground on the day of the 20th anniversary you could tell there were more people around than usual, but it was when we got inside the ground that it became clear just how many people had felt they needed to be at Anfield that day.

Everybody normally fits into the Kop stand for the service, but it had already been announced that the side stands would be open too. Not long before the start though, we saw stewards taking the netting off seats in the Anfield Road end as well so great were the numbers.

There must have been at least 30,000 there. Never before had so many people come to pay their respects to our 96.

The service was as beautiful and as painful as ever. Abide With Me, the reading of the names and the lighting of the candles, the minute's silence, the lovely Pie

Jesu, the prayers. And then came Andy Burnham MP.

He had always seemed alright for politician, the then Minister for Sport. Everyone knew he was a local lad, a massive Blue who had been at Villa Park watching the other semi-final on that day in 1989.

He had a message for us from the Prime Minister, Gordon Brown. And after all this time, with not even a sniff of justice, this was the best he could offer. "We can at least pledge that 96 fellow football supporters who died will never be forgotten." Everyone went mad. Mum explained...

'The shouting seemed to start near us. 'JUSTICE FOR THE 96'. It started to get louder and louder. I looked across at the players and the families as we were on the same row. Nobody was saying a word.

I started to think 'This is perhaps not the day to do this, we are here today to remember our 96'.

But as the chanting got louder, I started to feel the adrenaline rise from my feet going to my head. I started shouting with everyone else, thinking 'This needs to be done!'

I looked at Andy Burnham. He just stood there and took it. I felt a bit sorry for him, but I was glad it happened. It made me feel good. Justice was what we wanted, and deserved, and this felt like it could be a turning point in our fight. We had let the government know that we were not going away.'

Andy Burnham had agonised over that service. First of all over whether he should go to the service at all and secondly over what he should say.

"It gets a bit lost over the passage of time, but Maria Eagle and I had called for full disclosure of all Hillsborough documents a few days in advance of me going," he recalls.

"We were sticking our heads over the parapet a touch, there was no government cover for saying it, but there had been a piece in The Guardian a couple of weeks before about the amending of police statements, coming from the material which had been deposited in the Lords following the Stuart-Smith inquiry, which Maria had been instrumental in securing.

"It was Steve Rotheram who had invited me to go to the service. I didn't really know Steve properly until 2008, but over the course of the Capital of Culture year, with him as Lord Mayor and me as Culture Minister, we spent a lot of time together and became good friends.

"I remember sitting in the Anglican Cathedral with him about a month beforehand at the funeral of Gary Dunne, a 22-year-old Liverpool builder whose body we'd had to work hard to persuade Spanish authorities to allow be brought home after he had been tragically killed on the Costa del Sol.

"Steve kept saying, 'You've got to go to the 20th anniversary service, you're someone who is in a position to try and do something about Hillsborough now.'

"All the government briefings were that I shouldn't go and they tried to talk me out of it, but I just knew I had to.

"In consciously rejecting that advice and writing my own speech, the product of a few long and late discussions with my brothers, I knew I was putting myself out there, but I felt I had to plant the seed that we were trying to do something, even if we weren't in a position to shout it from the rooftops.

"So I went, but with a certain degree of foreboding. With the arrival of this landmark anniversary, it did feel like things were reaching a critical mass.

"I could not have predicted that it would pan out the way it did when I got up to speak in front of the Kop, but I thought something might happen in the context of all that was going on at the time. Looking back now it was the best thing that could have happened."

Stevie Hart was sitting next to Mum and he was shouting as loudly as anyone, having been screwed over by so many different governments.

Jack Straw in particular had promised us the world, but didn't deliver anything. He badly let us down.

So when Andy Burnham got up and started talking about the Prime Minister and his empty words, Stevie thought to himself, 'That doesn't mean anything. You've done nothing for us.'

Fair play to Andy Burnham, though. It can't have been easy for him. A lot of people were not booing him as such. It was what he represented, and the way we had all been treated for such a long time.

Mum met Andy Burnham after the service. It was one of the things she wrote about:

'We all went back to The Albert afterwards for a quick drink and then I had to make my way to the Town Hall as the families had been awarded the Freedom of the City of Liverpool.

It was a lovely service with the Lord Mayor Steve Rotheram giving a speech and we all received a scroll. I was talking with some people, including Kenny Dalglish, when Andy Burnham came past.

I pulled him and told him what I thought. I said to him, "When you get the truth out, you will find there are two police forces responsible for the cover-up of Hillsborough: South Yorkshire for their lack of care and West Midlands for changing witness statements to protect the first lot. Go back and tell Jack Straw."

I gave it to him straight. I made my points pretty strongly. He listened and said he would try to do something about what I was saying.

There had been stories in the media not long beforehand about potential changes to the '30-year rule' regarding the release of official documents. He said he was going to talk to his fellow ministers about releasing the relevant papers on Hillsborough early.

I didn't really believe that would happen after all we had been through with the Stuart-Smith stitch-up and Jack Straw, but Burnham seemed genuine. He was interested in what I had to say and did seem to know some of the details of Kevin's case.

On the way home, I started to think maybe it would have been better if I hadn't had a go at him, but it was too late. It was done, it was the truth and it worked.'

Peter Carney was with Mum when she gave Burnham what for.

She'd asked him to go with her for the Freedom of the City ceremony and he had a lot of running around to do to make sure that the new Hillsborough banner he'd made for the 20th anniversary was taken down from where it was hung in Anfield during the service and brought along into town. But he wouldn't have missed it for the world.

He told me that Mum collared Burnham in a doorway of the big hall upstairs in the Town Hall and basically badgered him. Told him that he had to give her a new inquest into Kev's death.

Peter tried to reinforce what she was saying. He told him that a new inquest was the very least she deserved and that he had the power to help her get it.

Burnham was genuinely inquisitive, if a little shaken, but seemed on the level and promised he was going to go back to Westminster and do everything he could.

"Coming away from Anfield after the service, my mind was filled with what I had to do next," revealed Burnham.

"It had been a difficult experience, but it was so clear to me now that I really had to go for it.

"Steve Rotheram came up to me and said, 'Don't go home, come to the Town Hall and speak to the families.'

"I really didn't know if I should, but he was insistent and he was so right.

"I'd been aware of Anne's case for some time and knew her petition to the European Court of Human Rights had just been refused, but this was the first time I became fully aware of the enormity of what she was doing.

"I remember her looking me in her eye and saying 'I know Kevin was alive' before going through all the evidence she had uncovered and asking me if I knew the various legal avenues she'd been down.

"The way she put her case across to me was compelling, with such clarity and a real, dignified persistence. She really got through to me.

"It was an unforgettable day with so much having happened and I remember going home thinking about it all, just trying to take everything in, but my conversation with Anne was what stuck with me most of all.

"She had spoken with such certainty that it hammered home to me again that there was so much that was utterly wrong with Hillsborough and needed to be confronted.

"When I reflect now, looking her in the eye and promising her I was going to do everything I could to make full disclosure happen was the moment I was committing myself emotionally, intellectually and wholeheartedly to the fight for justice."

Within days, Andy Burnham came through for us.

It was announced that all the documents held by the police, the ambulance service, West Midlands Police and other public bodies involved with Hillsborough would be made publicly available, ten years ahead of their scheduled release.

We knew it wouldn't happen overnight, but at the end of that year the Hillsborough Independent Panel was set up to manage it all.

They reckoned it could take about two years to sort through it all, which was frustrating when we thought about how long we'd already been waiting, but at least something was happening. We were promised that the families would be involved in the process and would get to see everything first, which was important to us.

It was good as well to see the people they brought in to be on the Panel.

It was going to be led by the then Bishop of Liverpool James Jones, who had done lots of work behind the scenes to help get Michael Shields released from prison, and there were other people that we knew had done good work on Hillsborough like professor Phil Scraton, who had done a lot of research down the years, and Katy Jones, who had been part of Jimmy McGovern's team for the TV drama back in 1996.

So we just had to be patient and wait. Again.

All the different groups met with the Panel and I remember when Mum came back from her first meeting with them, she was very wary. She had been thinking about resubmitting to the Attorney General after what had happened with Europe, but the lawyers advised we should wait and see what the Panel came up with.

Mum was asked to submit all her evidence to Bishop James and his team, but she had done that with Stuart-Smith and look what happened there. She was reluctant to give them anything at first because she was worried about another stitch-up, but after a few more meetings she was encouraged by how nice they were and that many of the families knew most of them so she handed everything over.

We got the odd update, but they didn't tell us much. They kept saying all the information they dug up had to be released at the same time so it would have a bigger impact. It made sense, I suppose, but didn't make us any less impatient to know what was going on. We tried to keep awareness ticking over with fundraising events here and there, but things were quiet. And then, suddenly, Hillsborough was all over the news again.

It came out that the BBC had been waiting two years for a response about a Freedom of Information request put in just after the 20th anniversary for documents about the private briefings Margaret Thatcher had with various people in the first few days after the disaster. We always thought she must have had something to do with the cover-up.

The Information Commissioner, Christopher Graham, ruled that the papers must be released straight away and criticised the length of time it had taken for the request to be dealt with, but the government then appealed the decision, saying everything should be sent to the Independent Panel first.

Someone called Brian Irvine started up one of the government's own e-petitions calling for all Government documents to do with Hillsborough to be released and within days it had 100,000 names on it, meaning that they had to at least consider having a debate about it in Parliament. Soon after it was confirmed that would happen, on Monday, October 17, 2011.

We had all signed it and it was fantastic to see that after all this time people still cared.

Mum wanted to go down to London for it, but we were a bit confused over what was happening as we'd heard that lots of the families thought the Thatcher documents should go straight to the Panel rather than the BBC.

She went to see her MP Stephen Mosely the Friday before and he confirmed the Panel would get them first, but it was still good news and worth going because it was building momentum and keeping Hillsborough in the spotlight. So she did.

Mum came home quite pleased with what had gone on. The Home Secretary, Theresa May, promised that everything would go to the Panel with nothing being left out and there was a lot of support from all the MPs who spoke.

Quite a few of them mentioned Kev and made a lot of the points about 3.15pm and the covering-up of important evidence. Exactly what Mum had been been saying for years.

Steve Rotheram, who was now MP for Walton, read out the names of the 96 so they would be recorded in Hansard forever and no-one was left in any doubt about just how strongly people still wanted justice.

We knew it would still be months before the Panel were ready to deliver their report so the next day Mum decided to strike while the iron was hot. She wrote down how it all happened:

'I read up about e-petitions and decided to start one for Kevin. It asked for the Attorney General to give him a new inquest under Section 13 of the Coroners Act.

There were three time options you could choose

for when it had to hit its target by. Three months, six months or a year so I chose the shortest one, thinking that was all we would need after how well that last one had done. I posted it on my Facebook page and people started to sign it straight away.

It moved quite well at first, but then seemed to stop. I felt a bit silly thinking people would be interested in signing a petition for Kevin to get a new inquest. Maybe everyone had had enough of Hillsborough for a while.

Then, shortly after Christmas, I was invited to a game by the lads from the Poor Scouser Tommy website who had done some fundraising for Hope For Hillsborough and had a cheque for us.

Kevin Reavey, who ran the Scouser Tommy site, asked about the e-petition and I told him how there was only about a week to go until the closing date and it was stuck on about 18,000 signatures.

He said he would try and get it some more publicity, but I didn't think there was any chance of getting more than 80,000 signatures in a week. But then it just seemed to snowball and the numbers started rocketing up.

I couldn't believe it. Twitter came into its own. Everybody started re-tweeting it – the Hillsborough Justice Campaign, Empire of the Kop, the Liverpool Echo, Liverpool Football Club themselves.

It was amazing just sitting there, looking at the page

and watching the numbers go up and up and up. Kelly Cates, Kenny Dalglish's daughter tweeted about it and then Kenny, who was Liverpool manager again by this time, did the same thing.

Our Sara was so excited. She texted me 'King Kenny's signed it!'...'

The support Mum got for the e-petition was amazing in the end. Loads of people helped give it a push on Twitter, but I think it was Kenny that helped tip it over the edge.

We made the deadline and got over 118,000 signatures, but then the Back Bench Business Committee turned it down for a Westminster Debate because of a "lack of time". That bloody expression again.

Eventually they decided they would have a debate about Kevin's inquest in Westminster Hall, which meant that the MPs wouldn't be allowed to vote on it. Not ideal, but it was better than nothing.

We travelled down the day before and it seemed to go pretty well. Lots of different politicians spoke about Kevin, what happened on the day and all the evidence that Mum had dug out about the cover-up. I sat there thinking 'how can you refuse us this time?'

It finished up with the Attorney General, Dominic Grieve, saying that he would have to wait until the Independent Panel's report, but he expected it to bring out more evidence that would help Kev's case so he would keep an open mind.

I was quite disappointed at first as I didn't under-stand exactly how it all worked. I had been hoping they would just award us the new inquest there and then. But Mum explained to me that it was still a big step in the right direction and she was happy with how it went. That was the main thing and lifted my mood.

It was now just a case of waiting for the Panel.

It had been frustrating when we were told the release of their report was now going to be in the September, rather than the spring as earlier forecast, but what was another few months when we'd already been waiting so long?

Momentum was building – it certainly felt like it was building more than at any other time in the past 23 years – but we'd had too many false dawns to count on anything.

All we could do was hope and pray that, this time, things would be different.

13

Moment Of Truth

'I'm delighted the report has once and for all set the record straight about our Liverpool fans'

St George's Plateau, outside St George's Hall, will always have significance for fans of Liverpool Football Club.

It was there where many successful Liverpool sides returned to on their homecoming after winning a piece of silverware. The crowds that swarmed around the area after the Reds won the European Cup in Istanbul in 2005 had to be seen to be believed. It didn't feel like half the city was there. It felt like it was half the world.

Upon those steps the great Bill Shankly addressed Liverpool supporters on more than one occasion. In

1971, after Liverpool had lost the FA Cup final to Arsenal, thousands of fans still turned up to welcome the team back to Merseyside.

Shankly stood there, his arms held aloft, and told the crowds "It's questionable if Chairman Mao of China could have arranged such a show of strength." The place erupted. They hung on his every word. It was a remarkable scene.

Over 40 years later, in a very different way and for a very different reason, Mum would stand on the same steps and make a dramatic, powerful speech of her own.

"Justice. What a lovely word. I hated it for 23 years."

That was the way she started her speech, stood in front of thousands of people and with several TV cameras pointing at her, in reaction to the findings of the Independent Panel's report on September 12. Truth Day.

Speaking confidently and happily she continued: "The report was excellent. I was wary of the Panel at first after what happened with Stuart-Smith and the way we got stitched up there. But I got to know them over time and they looked after us, they really seemed to care.

"They came to see me a few times to get documents and evidence for their report. I'd not been well for a few months, although I'm on the mend now. They were lovely, always asking how I was and saying things like 'You get yourself better, Anne'.

"They were so kind to us that over the last year I did start to feel more confident that they would do us justice. But I didn't know the report would be as strong as it was. For the first time it felt like they were finally listening to us.

"The thought of waking up in the morning and thinking 'I can do what I like today, I don't have to do anything on Hillsborough' is nice. I've always been sorting through documents and submitting files. I'm sick to death of files.

"I just want to be able to say 'I've done it now. Kevin's got his death certificate, he's at peace and I'm at peace'.

"I can't wait until I can put my little boy at peace because I want a life."

I thought back to it being Finlay's birthday. Mum said it had been an omen.

She told the press: "We're all getting older. I've got two other lovely children and they've given me three grandchildren.

"My daughter's youngest, Finlay, was four today and he's the spitting image of Kevin. I think God's given me Kevin back in this little boy.

"We always thought that perhaps with it being released on Fin's birthday it would be a good omen for the Panel's report and I think it was. We'll never forget Finlay's fourth birthday now.

"It was good to hear David Cameron admit that we've suffered a double injustice which is something I've always said. We lost our children and to go through something like that is the worst thing that can happen to you. Your whole life is turned upside down. And then you have lies and the cover-up so you can't even grieve properly. So there was always two issues to deal with, which is cruel.

"I'm delighted the report has once and for all set the record straight about our Liverpool fans. They were not to blame. They saved lives that day.

"They did the evacuation themselves while too many other supposed professionals stood around doing nothing. The police kept the ambulances outside the ground and told the drivers the fans were still fighting while in fact they were dying at their feet.

"You get sick over the years of trying to explain to people that the fans were heroes on the day and then you hear all the lies that some idiots still believe. Robbing the dead. How could they have done? They didn't have time, they were too busy trying to save them.

"God knows how many more would have died, but for them."

Many of the survivors and campaigners who had supported Mum were delighted for her. They were delighted for everyone affected by Hillsborough, but they knew how much Mum had been through to get to this point.

LIVERPOOL ECHO

5pm SPECIAL EDITION

www.liverpoolecho.co.uk

THE VOICE OF LIVERPOOL   40,976   HILLSBOROUGH LATE EXTRA   Wednesday, September 12, 2012   55p

Hillsborough
The Report of the Hillsborough
Independent Panel

41 COULD HAVE BEEN SAVED

Victims of wholesale blunders
Police altered 164 statements
and tried to smear the dead
Families: 'We're vindicated'
Cameron: 'We're sorry'
Law chief to rule on new inquests

REPORTS AND REACTION – PAGES 2,3,4,5,6,7,8,9,10 & 11

Peter Carney attended the press conference at Liverpool's Anglican Cathedral with her. He was sat by Mum's side when she took questions. It's something he'll never forget.

"I'd never seen Anne so easy in herself in all the time I'd known her," he recalls. "She had a glow that day.

"I remember sitting on the podium next to her during the press conference in the Cathedral, smug almost, just thinking, 'Tell them. Tell them again. Have your day, girl.' When she told them it was her grandson's birthday, I hugged her.

"Listening to David Cameron earlier made me think that this country had missed a trick. Liverpool supporters performing the rescue that day was the finest example of spontaneous humanity that this country's ever witnessed. Yet they never got onto it.

"They were too busy blaming the victims and covering the backs of those that caused the disaster and should have carried out the rescue.

"It was special to be with Anne at the Cathedral after all we'd been through together. I was also honoured to be the one who drove her from the Cathedral to the St George's Hall vigil, just as I had taken her from the twentieth anniversary service at the ground to receive her Freedom of the City scroll at the Town Hall.

"Most of the families left the Cathedral in posh Premier League-style coaches with police outriders and everything, but because we were the last ones to speak to the press – and, let's face it, with Anne involved that was never going to be a short affair – they had already left by the time we finished.

"So my abiding memory of Anne on Truth Day will be of her sat amongst regular Reds in my big red 'Boogie Bus' campervan that we normally use to go to the away games.

"We were stuttering and spluttering through traffic jams, caused by road closures due to the vigil, giving Anne an open window bus tour through the city, and stopping off on the way to St George's Hall so she could get ciggy papers!"

Dean Harris, who also accompanied Mum to the Cathedral, was blown away by how the day unfolded.

"Along with meeting Anne, September 12, 2012 was the most important day of my life so far," he reveals.

"The survivors were given separate disclosure by the Panel from the families so I didn't see Anne at first, but when we did catch up her smile could have lit up the Cathedral. That building means as much to me as Anfield now.

"I think it took a while for it to all sink in for her. She had faced so many brick walls and had that many knock-backs that it must have felt quite unreal for her, as it did for me, but over the course of the day you could sense her coming to terms with it and it was so special to be able to share that with her.

"When she asked me to do her press conference with

her, I couldn't have been more proud. To be able to sit alongside her, knowing how hard she worked to make the day happen, with the eyes of the world on us was very humbling.

"The vigil blew me away as well. To see her there, deservedly victorious on the steps in front of the St George's Hall, with all those people cheering her was just wonderful. It makes me smile whenever I see pictures of that moment because I can hear her voice going, 'I told you I was right.'"

Stevie Hart had a camera crew following him around for Truth Day. They had phoned a few days earlier and wanted him in a hotel room watching it on television as it all unfolded so they could film his reactions.

He wasn't sure what to do, so phoned Mum. "Yeah, do it," she told him. So he did.

Stevie had his son with him and they watched David Cameron's speech in the hotel. Then it was up to the Cathedral to do a live interview in the pouring rain and back to the hotel for the Panel's press conference.

They wanted to carry on filming him at the vigil, but he admits he'd pretty much had enough by that point.

"I said to them, 'Everything's bubbling up here, I need a bit of time with my son to take all this in'.

"We went to the Big House by Lime Street for a pint and within five minutes there were people coming over saying they'd just seen me on the box and buying us drinks. It was all a bit overwhelming.

"My wife and all the kids arrived and we went over to St George's Hall. We had plans to go for a drink afterwards, but when it was all over I just needed to get home. I just felt shattered, physically and emotionally drained. Almost on the verge of collapse.

"I always thought I'd be out on the bender to end them all if things went our way with the Panel, but it just pulled everything out of me.

"Breakfast TV wanted me at Anfield for 6am the following morning, but there was just no chance. The phone never stopped ringing for days and it did take a while for everything to settle down.

"I was so pleased for Anne, though. It's hard to put into words what it meant to see her walking out onto the steps at St George's with that smile on her face.

"The reception she got from all the people gathered there was fantastic, but it was only what she deserved. What a woman."

Ian Barnes was also there on Truth Day and it was he who arranged for Mum to stay in a hotel the night before so that she didn't have to face the journey from Chester that morning.

It was a relief that she was able to be there. She'd been unwell for quite a while, but thankfully got out of hospital just in time.

The hotel were really helpful and let Mum use the staff entrance so Ian could have a car waiting for her.

Trying to save Kevin: Off-duty PC Derek Bruder gives Kevin mouth-to-mouth on the Hillsborough pitch as Johnny Prescott supports his head

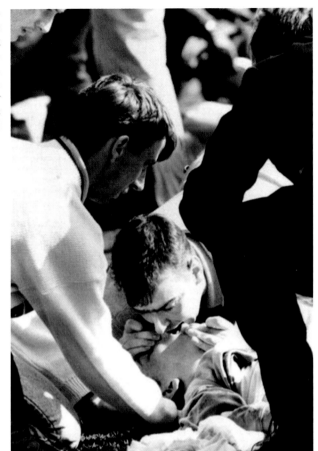

Helping hands: Stevie Hart (wearing white shirt and red scarf) and Tony O'Keefe (immediately behind him) carry Kevin across the pitch

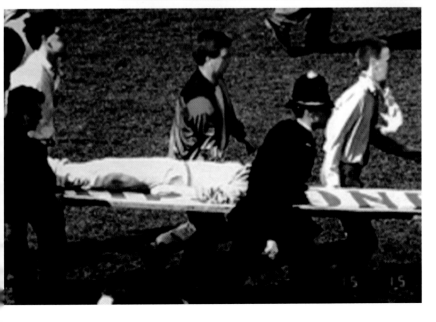

Justice for the 96: (Clockwise, from top) outside the Hillsborough Justice Campaign shop; Anne with Stevie Hart at the March 4 Justice, June, 2009; at a fundraising event in May, 2009; Anne and Ian Barnes with fundraisers Dougie Donnelly from Scouser Tommy and Pam Martin from Irish Kop in October, 2008

You'll never walk alone: Anne by the Shankly Gates and Hillsborough memorial

Peter's story:
Peter Carney,
standing in front of his
Hillsborough banner

Standing together:
(Left) Anne with John Glover, his son Thomas, Sheila Coleman and Carol Vorderman at 'This Is Your Life' for Ricky Tomlinson. (Below left) with Theresa Glover on the day Kevin's inquest verdict was quashed at the High Court

Good friends: (Below right) With Stevie Hart (red top) and John Herbert at a birthday party for Anne in February, 2013

Return to Hillsborough: Accompanying Stevie Hart (right) back to the scene of the tragedy in February, 2009. Above: At the memorial erected outside Sheffield Wednesday's ground

The fight goes on: (Clockwise, from top) Anne with Dean Harris (left) and Peter Carney at an HJC march; Francis Stanton presents Anne with a cheque after a Spirit of Shankly fundraiser in June, 2008; with Hope for Hillsborough founder member Ian Barnes and with Tony O'Keefe in London after Kevin's debate in February, 2012

Happy days: (Clockwise, from top) Anne's victory salute on Truth Day; brothers Danny and Chris; with nieces Stephanie & Heather and enjoying time with Finlay

With hope in her heart: Nothing would stop Anne from attending the memorial service at Anfield in April, 2013. Sitting next to her are Lena and (just behind) Sara

Saying goodbye: Crowds line the route as the funeral procession makes its way through Formby; Liverpool manager Brendan Rodgers and the club's managing director Ian Ayre pay their respects; the family's floral tribute; a sign in Waterloo sums up the feeling in the city towards Anne and (right) the Lime Street media wall on the day of the funeral

Iron Lady: Big Reds fly their flag (top) during the Reds' friendly against an Indonesian XI at Jakarta's Gelora Bung Karno stadium in July, 2013 and the flag makes it home to the Kop (above). Left: the Hope For Hillsborough banner

Kevin's team:
Sara with the European Cup.
Kevin would have loved
the way the Reds won the
trophy in Istanbul in 2005.
Right: Finlay kicks off the
memorial game between
the Scouse Reds and the
Norwegian Wools in
September, 2013

Carrying on the fight:
Sara with Finlay and Lena under
the Shankly statue at Anfield

He took on the responsibility of making sure she got to interviews and meetings on schedule.

"Anne could talk a glass eye to sleep at the best of times and there was plenty to get through that morning, but we got up to the Cathedral," Ian recalls. "I remember standing outside with her as she had one last rolly before we went in.

"She was hopeful, but not particularly confident, of what the Panel's report would say. I remember saying to her, 'No matter what happens today, you've got to be proud of how you've fought for Kevin and how far you've come. Who would have thought you'd be here a few years ago?'

"We went in and sat right near the front. One of the things that always stuck with me was when they said how different things could have been if they'd just used one word. Catastrophe.

"That's all they had to say over the police radio to set a recovery plan into motion, but they never did. And I just thought: 'how could this happen? Am I living in England or some third world country?'

"I am one of those people who grew up with a fair amount of faith in the institutions of this country, the justice system and so on, and even though Anne had told me plenty down the years about the lies and the corruption Hillsborough was riddled with, I was still shocked.

"Anne's reaction was quite calm, though. It wasn't

a shock to her because much of what the Panel revealed was things she had been saying for a long time, although I think even she was a little surprised at the scale of it.

"Before we went to St George's Hall she said she was a bit nervous at having to speak at the vigil, but I just told her to focus on one person in the crowd and concentrate on them.

"She was magnificent. To see her finally being taken seriously and get cheered to the rafters, after people had thought she was barmy for so long, was something I'll never forget."

Tony O'Keefe wasn't able to make it up to Liverpool, but followed it all on the TV.

"Seeing the pictures of her on St George's Hall reminded me of Bill Shankly and the famous speeches he gave on the very same spot," he says. "I do think she has been the same kind of inspirational figure.

"Anne has been a leader for people in times of such darkness and moved them by her example. She kept going for all those years and there must have been so many times when she must have thought 'what's the point?'

"But it paid off in the end, not just for Kevin but for everybody, and that's why people will always remember her."

As for Dave Kirby, the doubts he had about whether

the whole truth about Hillsborough would come out in his lifetime disappeared when the Panel revealed their findings.

"I used to say to my kids, who are grown up now, that I hoped the truth about Hillsborough would come out in my lifetime but, if it didn't, maybe it would in theirs.

"That's why I made sure they were always clued up on what happened because, to be honest, I doubted whether I'd be around to see it.

"You can't underestimate how massive that day was for us. I was planning to go into the Cathedral, but I couldn't in the end. I was so tense and nervous I just stayed in the car, parked on Hope Street, listening on the radio. It was like one those JFK 'where-were-you' moments when the details started to flood out.

"And it was a good job I was on my own because of the emotions and the pent-up frustrations that came flooding out. There was a lot of tears, but I was elated and angry as well.

"I remember punching the steering wheel because it really felt like we'd smoked the bastards out of their holes and they couldn't hide any more.

"I'd only been involved in the campaign for about 15 years and that's what that day did to me so I can imagine what it must have meant to Anne and the other families who had been fighting for even longer.

"I took my wife and kids down to the vigil and it was one of those amazing communal experiences that sum

Liverpool up in many ways.

"If Hillsborough had happened to someone else maybe the truth would never have seen the light of day, but that was never an option with us. Even if it took some time.

"Rodgers and Hammerstein wrote 'You'll Never Walk Alone' in 1944, but that song describes the attitude Anne and many like her wore on their sleeves when they were walking in the wilderness for nearly a quarter of a century. Liverpool's anthem had more meaning that day than ever.

"Anne never believed she was walking alone, even if it must have felt like it at times. That burning passion she had for the truth is what we need to keep tapping into to get justice because the race is not run yet."

Andy Burnham, who played such a big part in setting the wheels in motion at the 20th anniversary service three years earlier, was overwhelmed by the whole day. He described the tension and emotion he felt the night before as "almost unbearable," and was full of praise for Mum's efforts.

"It was a team effort and Anne played an utterly crucial role," he says. "I'll never forget seeing her at St George's Hall. We had a lovely conversation and I was so pleased for her and everyone else that the conviction and determination they had displayed for so many years was finally being recognised.

"People will look back on Hillsborough as one of the

most astonishing chapters in British social history. It will come to be seen as emblematic of a story that goes to the heart of how power between the classes was distributed and challenged.

"You can draw a comparison with Peterloo and how working class people fought back for what they believed was right.

"Throughout history injustices like Hillsborough have been allowed to ride and nobody's batted an eyelid, but this will be seen as a moment when the hierarchical structures of our country were challenged and shaken fundamentally.

"It was hard to see at times how they could possibly prevail given where they were at various dark moments, but they did because they just refused to be beaten and because of the strength of character Anne and the other mums showed.

"Anne, and those other mums, will forever be an inspiration for any mother fighting for their child."

Like Mum, Sheila Coleman, representing the Hillsborough Justice Campaign, also gave a press conference and spoke on the steps of St George's Hall.

She and Mum had sadly lost touch by that point – Hillsborough put a strain on so many relationships, many of them formed as a result of what happened in 1989 – but they rekindled their friendship that day.

"It was a ground-breaking day in the fight for justice, a real turning-point, but it could not have happened without the solidarity and strength in adversity that our city is famous for," Sheila says.

"People remained ignorant of the facts for so long because they were told lies. It was only through the dignified and vociferous perseverance of families, survivors and supporters that the cover-up was finally unearthed.

"Anne and I had sadly lost touch, but we chatted for the first time in years that day.

"I was so pleased to have my friend back after all we had been through together. She didn't look a bit well, though.

"I'd heard she'd been in hospital and I could tell how ill she was. She looked like my own mum did when she was dying. I told her to look after herself and get properly checked out.

"A few days later she rang me saying her barrister had advised that it would make sense for her to join up with the Hillsborough Justice Campaign again. I agreed completely. This was a time for unity and for us all to be working together to make sure that justice followed the truth.

"I could hear the relief in her voice when I told her that. I think she knew how ill she was. I'll always remember her words, 'I'm so glad I can pass it onto you.'

"We agreed to put the past behind us and I said to her, 'I'll do it on one condition: that you go to the hospital and get yourself sorted out because you're not well.'"

Being totally honest, we didn't have much faith in the Panel at the start and, after everything that had gone before, could you blame us?

We just thought they had been brought in to shut us up.

There was so much hope and expectation in the build-up to the report that I thought it was inevitable that we would end up disappointed. There was never going to be a big smoking gun pointing at the guilty, but it categorically placed the blame where we knew it always was.

So it was fantastic that, finally, everyone could see that Mum did know what she was talking about and had been right all along.

I honestly believe she would have found another route to go down if things hadn't worked out because she just didn't know how to give up on Kevin and Hillsborough.

But she was tired of constantly swimming against the tide and, as she was soon to find out, she now had another massive battle on her hands...

14

Time To Say Goodbye
*'I've waited 23 years for this. I thought I
wouldn't get it...but it's all been worth it'*

TRUTH Day had gone better than any of us could
have hoped to expect.

All the waiting and all the worrying seemed worth it
when the Independent Panel delivered the verdict that
finally established the truth about Hillsborough, sent
the Establishment scurrying for cover and vindicated
Mum for all those years of blood, sweat and tears.

She looked almost invincible as she stood there on St
George's Plateau.

We all hoped it would be a big boost on her road to
recovery. But once the adrenaline wore off, the pain

232

was back with a vengeance. It hit her hard. She was so looking forward to seeing the job through to the end, it just seemed so cruel that she had got ill. The bowel complaint had been masking the real problem.

Cancer.

I think she knew all along, to be honest. I could just sense it.

I was with her in the room when she got told the cancer was terminal. It was towards the end of October, just over a month after Truth Day.

She just sat there and took it. I was in pieces.

Mum was quite calm about the whole thing, like it wasn't a surprise to her. Like she'd been expecting the worst. Another blow. But one not even she could pick herself up off the canvas from.

She said straight away she didn't want to know how long she had left. She just wanted to get on with life. With enjoying her family. With carrying on the fight for justice.

I suppose we shouldn't have expected anything else from her.

It almost didn't seem real to me for a while after that. It was always there in the back of my mind, but she seemed to be doing really well.

She said at one point, in the first few weeks, that she didn't think she'd make it to Christmas, but once the steroids started to do their work she was pain-free. She started to feel and look much better.

Mum was bouncing around again. Lena even said at one point, "Nanny's better now," and that's what it felt like. For a while.

Family had always meant everything to Mum and nearly everyone really rallied around, especially her brother Danny and his wife, my auntie Sandra.

Danny takes up the story...

"We knew, of course, that Anne had been unwell for months and we had all been worried about her.

"I hadn't heard from her for a few weeks in the build-up to the Independent Panel's report and then I got a call from her one Friday night while I was out having a pint in my local club.

"She rang to say she had had to go into hospital because she was still in a lot of pain and was struggling to walk or stand for any length of time.

"I knew she hadn't been in the best of health for the last 12 months and I was very concerned. I told her she could come and stay with us while her medication started to work and we kept in touch over the weekend.

"Thankfully she started to feel a little better. She was so determined to be in Liverpool on September 12.

"I spoke to her that morning to tell her that our Chris and I would be on the Plateau at St George's Hall to support her and Kevin. She asked us to come to the Cathedral as well, but I told her we'd just stay in the background. We arranged to meet up afterwards.

"Anne said she wasn't feeling too bad but, like us all, was very apprehensive about the findings. She actually said, 'We're probably going to get stitched-up again anyway,' but of course, in the end, we needn't have worried.

"We didn't get the chance to see her afterwards, unfortunately. As she later told me, once the adrenaline wore off she was in pain again and if it hadn't been for the Lady Mayor holding her up at times she would have collapsed. She went home as soon as the vigil ended.

"It was a wonderful moment, though, when she got up to speak in front of that huge crowd. She had been so courageous for all that time and it was good that people finally recognised that.

"We couldn't have been more proud of her.

"But after that day and before long she was in a bad way again.

"I kept telling her to come to us and she kept saying she'd see how things go. She tried to battle on, but finally she said she couldn't manage any more so I arranged to pick her up from Sara's.

"The first week, although she was in some pain, she was managing to eat and enjoyed Sandra's cooking, but the second week was a different story.

"She couldn't face any food and was in so much pain she had to decline an invitation by Liverpool Football Club to represent the family at a ceremony for the 96 before the match against Manchester United, the first game at Anfield since the disclosure of the Independent Panel report.

"Anne asked me and Michael to go in her place and they really pulled out all the stops to make us feel welcome and laid on some wonderful hospitality for us.

"Ian Rush and Bobby Charlton released 96 balloons on the pitch, which was very moving, and together with the atmosphere of the crowd and the mosaics all around the ground by the supporters, it made for a very emotional afternoon. It was just a pity it was one of those occasions that we weren't meant to win.

"The fact that Anne's health was deteriorating was very distressing for us all, so we rang her doctor in Chester to arrange an appointment. Sara took Anne back to her flat and stayed with her for the weekend.

"She was back and forth between the doctors and the Countess of Chester Hospital for the next few weeks before finally being sent in for more tests. This time the results came back that there was nothing more the doctors could do.

"Anne rang to tell us the bad news. She was so calm and dignified. We suspected she had an idea for a while.

"Sara, Lena and Finlay had already been to see her and Michael was calling later on. Chris and I dashed off to the hospital with Chris' daughter Heather. We just couldn't wait to hug her and be with her.

"Not long after we got there, Anne's friends, Ann and

Brenda, arrived and we ended up having a good chat and a bit of a laugh. Anne said later that it cheered her up. It was very hard for us all to hold back the tears, though.

"We were grateful to the consultant and the Macmillan nurse for arranging permission for Anne to be admitted to Queenscourt Hospice in Southport where she could be near her family. After a couple of days Michael, Sara, Lena and Finlay collected Anne from the hospital and got her settled in there.

"I was able to visit her every night while she was in the hospice as it was just down the road from my home. It was during one of these visits, not long after she'd been admitted, that I said to her how well she looked.

"'That's because I'm pain free,' she replied, 'I haven't been like that for over twelve months.'

"I'll never forget her face when she told me that.

"I broke down and asked why she didn't say anything to anybody sooner. She just said she hadn't wanted any fuss. That was Anne.

"The treatment she got in Queenscourt was second to none. Nothing was too much trouble, they were always so friendly and welcoming.

"After ten days they'd got her medication balance sorted and she was eating better so we were asked if we could take Anne home with us.

"Our home was the obvious choice as Michael and Sara both had young families and it would have been very distressing for the children while Sandra would be able to look after her being home all day.

"We agreed without hesitation. She knew we were always there for her, but this was the first time she'd ever asked us for anything.

"In mid-November I brought Anne back to what was to be her new home.

"We soon got her settled back in and organised. She had her own room, which will always be known now as Anne's room, and her little routine each day, sitting in the garden under a covered area to have what she called 'a quick ciggy,' and watch the birds.

"Then she'd be on the couch in the living room to catch up with her friends on Facebook, make the notes that were to become the basis for this book and to watch telly with Sandra.

"She kept telling us how grateful she was to be with us and didn't want to be a burden. We reassured her and told her this was her new home now and to try to enjoy herself as much as she could.

"As things turned out, she was great company. Anne was always ready for a laugh and she loved a good chat. Her favourite programmes were all the soaps, The Chase and we used to fall about laughing at Mrs Brown's Boys.

"She was eating really well too, polishing off the lovely meals Sandra was making for her along with whatever else she fancied. Bowls of custard, bags of wine gums and especially Werther's Originals.

"An old friend, Sid, who was married to our cousin Maureen, was an old school pal of Anne's. He used to tease her rotten at school, but they got in touch when they heard about her illness to ask if they could come and visit her.

"Of course," I said, "she'll be made up to see you both," but Sid kept asking what he should bring her as a present? I told him there was no need to bother and he should just bring himself, but he was dead keen to take her something so I said that she was having a bit of a craze at the time for these Werther's Originals.

"Now Sid just happens to be a long distance lorry driver. "Oh right," he said. "I had a 40 foot trailer full of them the other day."

"The next day Sid turned up with a great big box full of them. Anne was delighted, although I think she must have started to get a bit sick of them after a while as half of them ended up in Sara's house for the kids!

"During her stay in the hospice and at home with us, Anne enjoyed the company of many visitors.

"She doted on her grandchildren Lena, Finlay and Grace and my grandchildren Andrew and Millie as well. It always gave her such a lift, watching the children play together and laughing about old times.

"Lots of people came by to see her and it was such a comfort to her.

"Stevie Hart texted her every single morning without fail, just to see how she was doing. Many of her Hillsborough friends paid visits along with old school pals, family we hadn't seen in years and even family we hadn't met before.

"Through Queenscourt, Anne received a message to contact our grandmother's niece, Wynne, who visited with her husband Ian regularly. Since then we've become quite close.

"It is a great pity that our mother and sister couldn't bring themselves to visit Anne before she passed away, neither in the hospice or at our home. Not even a phone call. We don't know to this day why. We all got Christmas cards except Anne and she was very hurt by that although she tried to put a brave face on it. As usual.

"As one of our cousins put it in a card she wrote after Anne died, 'If it wasn't for the adults in our lives, we'd have known each other a lot better'.

"We didn't know Kevin as well as we should have done because of the split in the family. We did see each other occasionally and always got on very well, but I did feel guilty about it. I told Anne how I felt and she said not to worry about it. But it hurt me. I suppose that's the way families are sometimes.

"We were determined to give Anne a good Christmas and that memorable day in London the week before when the inquest verdicts were finally quashed helped make it one that we'll never forget. Anne wanted so much to be there at the Royal Courts of Justice. This was what the three memorials to the Attorney General, the judicial review and the petition to the European Court of Human Rights had been about achieving. There was no way in the world she was going to miss it.

"So I organised a wheelchair and off we went. We travelled down by train the afternoon before and had a good night in the hotel with Stevie Hart, Ian Barnes and Charlotte Hennessy from Anne's Hope For Hillsborough group.

"It was good to meet Anne's legal team, Elkan Abrahamson and Pete Weatherby, who have been such magnificent allies and friends to her over the years.

"Even though she had the highest respect for them and everyone thought it was going to be a formality, Anne had been stitched up that many times before she still worried whether it would actually happen.

"Thankfully, though, justice was finally done. The accidental death verdicts were struck off and the Attorney General Dominic Grieve announced there would be new inquests as soon as possible, staying behind in the court afterwards to speak to the families personally, which we appreciated.

"There was a barrage of reporters outside all wanting to talk to Anne and I was bursting with pride for her. It was very emotional to stand behind her chair and listen to her talk about what the day meant to her."

This is what Mum said...

'I've waited 23 years for this. There were plenty of times when I thought I wasn't going to get it, but it's all been worth it. I was never going to give up. The 3.15pm cut-off point was placed in order to secure the accidental death verdict and it did. They should have just given us the truth from the outset.

I'm delighted for Kevin and the other 95, but also all the survivors, who were always getting landed with the blame which was so unfair. I used to feel so sorry for them, having to carry the can for what had gone on when in fact they should have been getting praise for springing into action and trying to save lives. They should be given medals.

Having the city behind us was always a big help. The support of the Liverpool and Everton fans, the people of Merseyside and other kind people from all over the world, really helped to keep me going.

I'm very pleased that the extremes those people went to in order to cover up the truth are going to be addressed. They deserve everything that's coming to them. They didn't care about our 96.

They didn't care about the survivors. In Kevin's case, they tried to destroy the lives of professional people just in order to make sure they secured that accidental death verdict. So it's their turn now to pay for what they've done.

We've made history, haven't we. We've got that

verdict struck off and everyone can know that Hillsborough was not an accident. This is not the end, but hopefully we'll reach a point where families are able to move on.

We'll never forget, of course, but we've always had to deal with two issues because of the cover-up.

If they'd held their hands up at the beginning, we could have at least tried to get on with our lives, but I couldn't because of all the lies.

It's a good feeling, because they bounced me from one wall to the other, and I knew what they were doing. I thought 'They're trying to wear me down, but I'll wear them down before they wear me down'. And I've actually done it!'

Mum and Danny's journey back home was actually a little subdued. They were tired, but happy. I think everyone just needed a bit of time to reflect on the result and slowly take in the warm feeling of success.

"Anne had a lovely Christmas with all her children and grandchildren around her," continues Danny.

"She was always such an easy person to like, but it was very special to really reconnect with her like I was able to do in those last few months.

"Whenever I got in from work she would always ask, every night without fail, 'How did you get on today? Did you get done what you wanted to do?' And I'd always tell her I did, even if I didn't.

"Whenever I took her a meal, and she'd be sat there on the couch, she'd look up and the way she said 'Ooh thank you,' would have melted the hardest of hearts.

"Anne would never go to bed without saying 'goodnight' and giving us a kiss. It sounds daft, but it meant a lot to us at the time. It means even more now.

"Occasionally, when she felt up to it, we took Anne to The Crown pub nearby for tea. No matter what the weather was like, once she made her mind up she was going she was happy to be pushed along in her wheelchair.

"On one occasion I hit the kerb and nearly tipped her out of her chair. I got the biggest telling off I've ever had. The air was blue! I certainly made sure I never did that again. She never ate very much. Scampi and chips followed by ice cream was her favourite.

"Every time we got back she would say, 'I enjoyed that, it was nice to get out for a bit.' Sandra and I used to wait for her to say that and have a little smile to ourselves. She was so easy to please.

"As we got towards spring, Anne's health gradually deteriorated to the point where she was very weak and unable to do a lot for herself. I could see it was taking its toll on Sandra. She would never complain, but reluctantly we asked a care nurse to come in each morning. They were all very kind and so thoughtful in helping Anne retain some dignity.

"In March, Anne suffered another setback on hearing

the news that her good friend and fellow campaigner for many years, John Glover, had passed away.

"She was so sad and upset that she was too ill herself to attend his funeral to be with Theresa and the rest of the Glover family as they had been friends for many years.

"About five days before the unveiling of the Hillsborough Justice Campaign monument on April 14, and the anniversary service at Anfield the next day, we had to send for Dr Kilshaw as Anne had become so weak.

"He had always been so good with her and during his visit Anne expressed how important it was for her to attend those two events. He arranged for her to return to Queenscourt for a blood transfusion to try and give her a bit of a boost.

"They all did their utmost to help get Anne there, we will never be able to thank them enough.

"Sadly Anne was too frail to attend the ceremony in Liverpool on the Sunday and was really upset. She felt she'd let Sheila and her friends down.

"Later that afternoon, Anne's barrister Pete Weatherby called in to see her on his way home from the unveiling. As always we were very glad to see him.

"He told us how well everything had gone and wanted to pass on everyone's best wishes to Anne.

"He said he was only stopping for ten minutes and ended staying for a couple of hours with us all sitting outside in the sunshine, chatting away. I don't think

Pete realised what a lift that visit gave Anne and the family. I hope he does now after reading this.

"That evening we were still doubtful whether Anne would be able to attend the anniversary service the following day. In my heart I was hoping she wouldn't go as I would be worried so much about the strain she was putting on herself, but I had promised I would do anything she wanted and I wouldn't go back on that.

"The next morning the nurse arrived as usual and got Anne up and dressed. I asked her how she was feeling?

"She just turned around and said, 'I'm going...if I can do anything with these bloody grey roots in my hair!'

"We managed to get hold of some dry hair colour, which Sara applied, before doing her make-up. Anne's feet and ankles had swollen up so she had to borrow Sandra's boots and once she was sorted I carried her into a cab kindly provided by ITV.

"She did a short interview with them on the way to Anfield and it was heartbreaking to hear her say, 'I know this will be my last year. I just really wanted to try and get there. Not to say goodbye, because I'll be going to Kevin.'

"We arrived at the ground and managed to make our way through the crowds of well-wishers and into The Albert to see the rest of the family: Chris, Michael, Sara, Lena, Finlay and Paul.

"Many of Anne's friends who she had battled with for so long to get justice came over and everyone was very pleased she had made it.

"This was the 24th memorial service, but the first one since the truth, the truth that she had done so much to bring to light, was finally accepted by the world outside of Merseyside.

"It meant so much to everyone to have her there although probably not as much as it meant to Anne. It was so moving to see people hug and make a fuss of her – and then turn away to cry.

"We all then went into the ground, going in by the side entrance because of Anne's wheelchair, and entered the Kop to a standing ovation.

"People were clapping her and calling her name. It was another very emotional moment, I have never experienced anything like it before.

"The service went well. It was just a pity that the organisers didn't acknowledge the effort Anne had made to get there like the families did.

"We were getting more concerned towards the end as Anne was so weak she was struggling to sit up straight in her chair. I asked her if she was ok and she just said, 'can we go home now?'

"Again, as we left, the families stood and clapped.

"We tried to head back to the cab, but were once again inundated with people wanting to speak to Anne. There were close friends who hadn't managed to catch her beforehand, supporters who recognised her and wanted to wish her well, people from all over the world.

There was one fellow from Australia who was very keen to meet her.

"I was so stressed and concerned to get Anne home that it was all a blur, but I know how glad she was to have made it to Anfield on the day. She was very tired, but she still managed to find the strength to give another interview, thanking the survivors and everybody who had helped over the years.

"Anne spoke beautifully. She never wanted to miss an opportunity to shout for justice for the 96.

"Sadly, the exertion of going to the service took as much out of her as we feared it might and by the next day she was slipping in and out of consciousness.

"She had regular visits from the family and we all had to smile when she woke up at one point and asked the doctor for 'half a lager and a ciggy,' before going back to sleep. She was left in no doubt how much we all loved her.

"On Thursday, April 18, at 2.10am, Anne passed away peacefully holding my hand. She didn't want to die alone and she didn't.

"We take comfort in the happy times that we shared and the many lovely words said by those whose lives she touched.

"Anne went through more than her fair share of bad times, even before Hillsborough and losing Kevin, but it never made her hard-hearted or bitter against life.

"She took people on face value and if she liked you,

you'd cracked it. If she didn't, or you crossed her, you'd be wasting your time because she'd just tell you!

"It was very difficult for us all to say goodbye to her. There was a service in celebration of her life at Our Lady of Compassion Church, the same church where she was christened and married, and where a memorial candle for Kevin has burned since 1989, before cremation in Southport.

"We asked Stevie Hart to give a reading at the service as he had always been such a wonderful friend to Anne. A poem called The Farewell was sent to us by an Irish writer called Peter Makem and it felt very fitting for Stevie to play a part in the service."

Stevie continues: "It was a huge honour and I was so proud that the family asked me to do it because Anne obviously meant an awful lot to me. I was a bag of nerves though. The last thing I wanted to do was get up there and break down. So I practised and practised and practised.

"It was quite funny how it panned out on the day. Anne would have laughed her head off.

"I use separate glasses for reading and had put them in my wife's bag beforehand. I didn't bother with an order of service and all of sudden heard my name getting called so I was on.

"I went up there, trying to keep calm and not look at Brendan Rodgers or Ian Ayre, and got up to the pulpit only to realise I didn't have my reading glasses with me! So I had two options: go back to my seat and fish them out of my wife's bag or try and muddle through without them.

"Thankfully I'd printed it out on our computer at home and it was in fairly large type so I was able to see it, just about. Afterwards, sitting there and thinking about it, it just made me think how much she'd have loved that. Despite everything, Anne liked a grin as much as anyone."

She wasn't afraid of dying, my mum.

There was one point in her last couple of days when we were all there at Danny's house and she asked everyone to leave the room except me.

She took my hand and just told me simply that she knew she was going soon, but she wasn't frightened and she didn't want me to be either.

It was typical of her that at a time like that she would be thinking of how I was feeling and trying to make me feel better. Mum was my best mate as well.

I don't think I'll ever get used to her not being around. She's still the first person I want to tell when one of the kids does something funny and the first person I'd think to ring when I need someone to tell me everything's going to be alright.

I'm just glad we were so close. Not all mums and daughters are like we were, as she knew herself.

I said to her in the last few days that she was lucky in

many ways. Obviously, not because of what was happening to her, but in having so many people around her who loved her so much. She knew that and she really was at peace with everything by the end.

The day of the funeral was so hard for us, but we were all very proud to see how many people turned out to pay their respects. We took the exact same route from Our Lady's to the crematorium as we did for Kevin's funeral and there were people all round Formby village clapping as we went past, as well as hundreds outside the church.

We'll never forget her and it seems like lots of other people won't either.

Four days after she died, the club invited us to Anfield for the match against Chelsea. Before the match there were banners on the Kop saying 'RIP Anne, You'll Never Walk Alone' and the fans were singing, "One Anne Williams, there's only one Anne Williams..."

It meant an awful lot to us.

There are a few flags now in honour of her that they fly proudly on the Kop, one of which came all the way from Indonesia. Liverpool were over there for their pre-season tour and we couldn't believe it when we heard the supporters over there had made a flag, featuring her face and 'The Iron Lady', for her.

It was so kind of them to send it over to England for us. I think she'd get a big kick out of seeing her face alongside Bill Shankly, Bob Paisley and all the others in the crowd. Not bad for a mum from Formby.

There's a part of me, though, that feels supporters on the other side of the world should never have had to find out who she was. She should have been able to lead a normal, private life with the same ups and downs as anybody else, but she wasn't allowed to because of the disgrace of Hillsborough and the shameful cover-up afterwards.

Mum won her battle to get the truth, but we all owe it to her, our Kevin, the 96, John Glover and countless others to make sure that justice follows. It's already taken far too long.

It hit home to me again just how important it is that the fight carries on when the lads who put on the Scouse Reds v Norwegian Wools charity game for Mum in 2009 organised it again as a memorial match for her, just after the first anniversary of the Independent Panel's report.

It was hard to believe it was only twelve months since that day when Mum had stood triumphantly on St George's Plateau.

Now, a year on from the HIP report, the IPCC were asking survivors who had made statements to the West Midlands Police to contact them as it had come out that those ones might have been altered as well as the hundreds of officers' ones that were.

Speaking to some of them, I was struck by how raw Hillsborough still is. Having to relive what they went through brought it all flooding back, which also applies for those who are only giving statements for the first time now.

It will be even tougher when they're giving evidence at the new inquests and it is so important that they are given as much support as possible.

Everyone must stick together and look out for each other because we've come too far to let this slip now.

But that solidarity has always been there and it was very much on show for Mum's memorial match.

It really was a lovely day. The sun shone and there was a great turn-out of people at the Liverpool County FA in Walton Hall Park. With all the flags and banners people had made and brought along, the little stand there was turned into the 'Anne Williams Kop'.

Finlay got to lead the teams out and kick the game off, before I presented the trophy to the Reds after their 9-0 win. The Norwegian lads were terrific, though, and we're so thankful to them for coming all that way.

There was a do afterwards at the Taxi Club, near Everton's ground, and it was a great night.

Thousands of pounds were raised for Queenscourt Hospice and Hope For Hillsborough, just a couple of months after a fundraising golf day had been held to meet the costs of Mum's funeral.

Donations came in from as far away as Melbourne, Australia. People have been so kind.

It was great to see so many of her friends and family

There was live music and I don't think anyone who was there will ever forget the song 16-year-old singer-songwriter Dominic Dunn performed for Mum. It was called 'The Angel' and he had written it himself the day before. It was beautiful. There wasn't a dry eye in the house.

The next day, I was still trying to take it all in.

Looking through all the photos people had taken made me realise again just how many lives Hillsborough has touched.

It took me back to the promise I made to Mum that I would always keep on fighting. I won't let her down and I know you lot won't either.

Everyone who knew and helped Mum has our family's heartfelt thanks for what you did for her.

You can take comfort that you were part of her life and you kept her going.

We can't begin to name you all for fear of missing someone out, but you know who you are.

We will never walk alone, she will always be with us.
JUSTICE FOR THE 96.

What They Say About Anne

Danny Gordon, Anne's brother

Anne never gave up her relentless fight for Kevin, the other 95 and the survivors. Through all the setbacks and disappointments, she carried on with courage and determination. From a shy little girl with a cheeky smile to a lady with such selfless strength, we are all so proud of her.

Chris Gordon, Anne's brother

I probably didn't realise just how much she had done on Hillsborough at first but, having seen the unbelievable work she put in down the years, I was overjoyed for her when she was proved right after all that time. I can understand the satisfaction she must have felt having heard the rubbish that some people, even in Formby, used to say about the Liverpool fans. Anne was on cloud nine because she knew they had been heroes on the day and she proved it to everybody, politicians and all, in the end.

She tried to see the best in people and always had time for everybody. I remember as we drove from the church after her funeral service, people remarking how popular she was when they saw the large crowds all gathered outside the church.

I wasn't surprised. We used to laugh how she'd go shopping in the village and say she would be only half an hour but not tip in until about three hours later because she would just end up meeting everyone, having a chat and bouncing from one person to the next.

She wouldn't cut anyone short and always seemed to have a very laid-back, happy-go-lucky attitude to life, which makes you surprised in a way at the fights she took on and won. Anne's character, in a lot of people's eyes, will have been defined through the resilience she showed because of Hillsborough, but she'd always been like that and that's why we all loved her.

Mike Williams, Anne's eldest son
I always supported my mum throughout her fight for justice for my brother Kevin. I just found it difficult to

know the details of how he died. I loved my brother and often think of what he would have done with his life. He was a clever lad and wanted to be a journalist or a lawyer. A lot of my memories I have blocked out as they are often painful to remember. I am, and always will be, immensely proud of my mum throughout her fight for justice and her fight with cancer.

Even when she moved away from Formby, she would come back regularly to see us, and when my daughter Grace was born we used to enjoy going to Chester to visit her. She was always made up to see us and I think it helped give her a break from her campaigning.

Grace loved going to visit mum in Chester but there was always someone she wanted to see first…Sooty! Sooty was my mum's cat and was very old. Grace loved her as much as her nanny and it was always the same routine. We would arrive at the flat to say 'hi' to mum then Grace would disappear to find Sooty, who would always be hiding somewhere.

Mum would make me a coffee and we would be having a chat when Grace would reappear with a scratch on her hand that Sooty had done within ten minutes of us getting there. This would be the same routine each time we visited and Grace would return home with another scratch, proudly telling everyone that 'Sooty did it'. This never stopped her looking for the cat! Grace referred to mum as 'Sooty's nanny' and her other nanny 'from down the road'.

Sadly Sooty died not long before mum became ill. We never told Grace, only telling her that Sooty had run off to live with other cats but when mum died we told her Sooty had gone with her to heaven.

Grace turned five the same day that mum passed away. It was a difficult day for me. We knew mum was deteriorating but we never thought it would be that quick. We had made plans to visit Giggle's Gym in Birkdale for tea if mum felt up to it as she was looking forward to celebrating Grace's birthday with her.

Sadly it was not to be. The day was a mixture of sadness and trying to make the day special for my daughter and thinking about my mum. We still went to Giggle's that day and took Finlay with us. We had made the decision not to tell Grace her nanny had died until after her birthday so she could enjoy the day.

Grace still has her birthday card along with money given by Mum and is saving up for an iPad. Mum also bought gifts for all the children to be given to them when she died. Grace was also given a beautiful silver necklace with a heart on. She wears this with pride on special occasions.

The day after Mum's funeral, Grace saw the front page of the Mirror which had pictures of us alongside the headline 'Liverpool mourns hero'. She probably won't understand exactly what that means until she's a bit older, but when she does she'll be as proud of her as we've all always been.

Lena Williams, Anne's eldest grandchild
(Sara's daughter)

The first time I realised Nanny was quite well known was during assembly at school. We sometimes learn about Liverpool, and what happened at Hillsborough, and I felt very proud that the teachers talked about her and all the important work she had done. Every tutor group in our year had to choose an inspirational person to name their group after and Nanny was picked for one of them. I couldn't wait to tell my mum as soon as she got home and she was really pleased.

Nanny would sometimes tell me about what she was doing. I didn't always understand everything but I knew her and Mum were very sad about what happened to uncle Kevin, and that's why they kept trying to get justice. Every year in our school we have the Kevin Williams Cup and I was asked to present the trophy to the winners and a cheque for the money that we raised for the Hillsborough Justice Campaign. Nanny was very happy when everyone finally knew the truth but I'm very sad that she can't see justice as well. I hope that people will keep fighting to finish the job for her.

Me and my brother Finlay had such fun when we went to stay with her for the weekend. Fin loved going on the slides in the park near where she lived and if we ever wanted to make her laugh we would get him to dance for her. Nanny used to sing this really old song to him called 'Bimbo' by someone called Jim Reeves but she would change the words to 'Finbo' and he would bop about until we were all crying laughing.

Nanny could be strict sometimes if we wound her up. She would get cross if we were messing about when we were supposed to be going to bed, or if we didn't tidy up our mess. But she would never stay angry for long.

She would make us brilliant burgers and homemade chips. She was a very good cook. Mummy and Nanny used to ask me which of them makes the best spaghetti bolognese. I would say Nanny did but they were both nice. One time me and my friend were having a sleepover at her house and we couldn't get to sleep so Nanny made us scrambled eggs at half past one in the morning. Sometimes we'd just lie in bed watching films together and talking. We'll always miss her.

James Jones, former Bishop of Liverpool

Anne Williams will always stand as an emblem for the strength and courage of a mother's love. In spite of her health she was driven by an extraordinary determination to prove the truth about how and why Kevin died at Hillsborough.

What she did for Kevin she did for all the 96. Her passionate struggle remains an inspiration to all who care for truth and justice. She had a strong belief in the afterlife and a certainty that through her own death she and Kevin would be together for eternity. May they rest in peace and in the truth and justice of their cause.

Liverpool Football Club

The resilience that Anne Williams showed in her long fight for justice for Kevin inspired people in Liverpool and beyond. Fans as far away as Indonesia created banners in her honour – as they did on the club's pre-season tour of Asia in the summer of 2013 – demonstrating how her courage touched so many supporters.

Just as the Kop will always remember the feats of the club's greatest players, it will never forget Anne Williams' battle for truth.

Elkan Abrahamson,
Anne's solicitor for over 20 years

I hope Anne will be remembered as one of the heroines and guiding lights of bringing justice for the 96.

It's tragic that she hasn't survived to see the new inquests, but thank goodness she survived to see the HIP report and the Attorney General's quashing of the original accidental death verdicts.

The comforting thought about the inquests is although she won't get to see them, she knew they were going to happen and was in full possession of the facts about Kevin so could probably have learnt little new there.

The great irony of her case was that her whole argument was based on people having the right to know the truth of what happened, when she had in fact already known it herself for many years.

By the time the inquest verdicts were quashed, she didn't need a new one to tell her what had happened to Kevin as she was already well aware, but she wanted the record to be set straight.

There was a couple of times when I had a conversation with Anne saying 'look, there are no more legal avenues, I think we've done everything we can. You have to think about whether this is taking over your life – and if it will actually achieve anything'.

She understood that it was unlikely that the law was going to achieve anything, but it was more that she had to get the government to move. The way to do that was to use the law, to use publicity and to use politicians, and she really got that.

So, when we would be having these discussions about the likelihood of success, her argument was it keeps the story going and keeps pressure up. That's what she was trying to do and what she succeeded in doing.

Her contribution has been absolutely essential. I would go as far as saying that, without her, we wouldn't be where we are today.

It wasn't just that she was saying 'this is awful, you need to reopen the inquests'. She explained why and came up with the evidence, finding the witnesses and experts who would support her time and time again.

Although she could present it in emotional terms, her campaign was very analytical and objective as well.

She was utterly steadfast in the fight that she was

involved with for the best part of 25 years and remained very personable and non-confrontational which, bearing in mind the difficulties between the different groups, I think helped her keep going. She always had a keen sense of humour, which she was able to tease out of the worst of situations.

There's a younger generation of people affected directly or otherwise by Hillsborough who are now able to understand Hillsborough thanks to Anne's efforts.

They are in a position to pick the baton up now that her leg of the race, arguably the most arduous, has been run.

Pete Weatherby, QC

Anne was an ordinary woman living an ordinary life with her husband and young kids until the tragedy struck. From then on, Anne became an extraordinary woman fighting an epic battle and, unfortunately for the establishment, she was clever, engaging and determined.

She worked tirelessly to uncover what really happened to Kevin. To uncover the corruption and lies that had cheated all the victims, the bereaved and survivors of truth, justice and closure.

When she was ill, but before she was diagnosed with the illness that killed her, Anne told me that people saw her as this perpetual campaigner. She was proud of that and what she had achieved. But, in truth, there was another side to Anne away from the limelight. She had a close and loving family of whom she was immensely proud.

I saw her three days before she died and she wanted to know all the news about the new inquest and fresh investigations. She reminisced about talking to some senior police officer involved in the cover-up who was trying to fob her off. She had sat and listened, thinking to herself 'you'll give in before I do'. And she was right.

As we parted we both knew this would be our last meeting because she was so ill, but she made me promise to come and see her straight after the next court hearing to update her. Death wasn't going to get in the way of her fight for justice.

Sheila Coleman, Hillsborough author and researcher
Historically, Anne will be seen predominantly as a mother who fought for her child. That most primal of instincts is what gave her that strength that she may not otherwise have possessed. But I wish she'd never had to find it. She was an ordinary family woman who loved her children and lost one of them.

The enormity of the task she took on, fighting the British establishment tooth and nail, hit her very hard because there was an innocence and naivety about her. She had an extremely trusting nature which was abused and exploited at times, unfortunately.

The fact that she was able to get off her deathbed and

make it to Anfield to the memorial service just days before she died symbolised her inner strength.

I gave her a big hug and a kiss as I saw her off into the cab when Danny took her home and that's when it hit me that was the last time I would ever see her. It cut me in half. I wasn't just crying because I was knew she was dying, I was crying for what 24 years of Hillsborough had done to her.

Racing through my head were so many of the things that we had been through. The situations we'd faced. The scrapes we'd got ourselves into. The funny things. The sad things. The anger I felt at what people had done to her.

Anne's support for the survivors was so important. She was like John Glover in that regard. Not everyone was. Anne acknowledged that the survivors could tell her about what Kevin went through, but also how, but for their efforts, even more people would have died.

She managed to track down all of those people who tried to help Kevin and while it was upsetting for her it really mattered to her. And it became a two-way thing.

By her telling survivors that she didn't blame them, at a time when Liverpool fans were still thought by many ignorant people as being to blame for the disaster despite having long been exonerated by the Taylor Report, it helped assuage the guilt that lots of them still felt. Many of them kind of adopted her because of that.

Her grasp of all the medical, legal and political details

she forced herself to learn was phenomenal. She was absolutely meticulous and disciplined herself to study all hours of the day and night, doing her homework to make sure that she was prepared and able to argue the toss, and have a complete grasp of the issues at hand so she would be on the ball whenever someone was trying to pull the wool over her eyes.

To do all of that without any kind of real academic background, to read it, to understand it, all the time every word you're taking in reminding you of the worst pain ever inflicted on you...it's hard to believe someone could keep going through all that. But Anne did.

Through it all, she developed a capacity to take the good out of things and to live a life within all that.

Theresa Glover, Hillsborough Justice Campaign (lost 20-year-old son Ian in the disaster)

My husband John and Anne were very close in the early years. They used to get all the news and a bit of gossip from one another and have long, long conversations over the phone. They worked so hard together to tell people the truth about what had gone on.

We lost our son Ian at Hillsborough and it was John that brought her into the group of families that were looking to investigate what had happened as we already knew we wouldn't get any answers if we had to rely on the authorities for them.

John and Anne knew, virtually right from the start,

just how bad the cover-up was, but nobody would believe them. God bless them both, I know they'll both be looking down and saying 'We were right and now we're finally getting somewhere'.

We did have some good times together. I think we all needed a sense of humour doing what we were doing.

When we were all staying in London for the judicial review, there was a fire alarm in the hotel one morning and we all had to evacuate.

Poor Anne had to come rushing out in her dressing gown and I had to tell a load of tourists off for staring at her while we were waiting outside. We had a good laugh about it afterwards saying how people in Liverpool wouldn't gawp like that and would just have a joke about it.

Anne deserves every 'mother of the year' award going. We were never going to stop battling for Ian and Joe, but I couldn't have done what she did, learning about all the medical and legal details.

Three weeks before she died, Anne phoned us when she heard that John was near the end himself to see how he was. It's such a shame that John and Anne both went so quickly after the HIP report. Two of the people who had worked hardest to see the truth come out − they both deserved to see justice as well.

That's why I'll keep going. John fought so hard for the cause and I want to be there for him. We would have been married 50 years in April, not long before the 25th anniversary of Hillsborough. But I'm nearly 75 now. How much longer have we got to wait to get justice for our children?

Ann Adlington, Solicitor; Liaison Officer of the Hillsborough Disaster Working Party, Liverpool City Council

Ultimately, Anne's role will be seen as pivotal because she was the one person who never ever gave up.

She was a lone voice in the wilderness for an awful long time and carried on the fight when most of the families were resigned to the fact that legally they had nowhere else to go; but she still kept chipping away and chipping away. If not for her, we might never have got to the stage we are at now.

She embraced survivors and supporters in a way that the other groups hadn't because she knew from Kevin's case how the fans had valiantly fought to save lives and how traumatised it left them. She was always very slight and very thin, but had this incredible spirit and a lot more resilience than people assumed she had. I think that is key to how she got so far.

She had a relaxed, calm way about her and deliberately allowed people to underestimate her intelligence. She had a knack of lulling people into a false sense of security and the more knockbacks she got, the more she went forward.

Bereavement can give people a bitter edge, but it

never did for Anne. She was always compassionate and ready to share her knowledge and put people in touch. She had a real generosity of spirit, never egotistical and always interested in other people's stories.

Stevie Hart, Hillsborough survivor
Anne is proof that you can take on the system, right to the very top, and win. She had her son taken away from her and felt she'd never been given the truth of what happened, so had to go out there and find it out herself.

If your kid goes to a football match and doesn't come home, you shouldn't have to go searching yourself for what went wrong, why he wasn't treated properly, why people have lied to cover their own backs. At the very least she should have been given the full story.

She had support from many different people and did draw strength from that but I think she was a bigger influence on them than they were on her. She was a cornerstone for everyone else to look to and bounce off. She was such a phenomenal fighter and everyone rallied around her, believing that she would eventually get there. And she did.

Peter Carney, Hillsborough survivor
The continuum of life in the story of Hillsborough is down to Anne Williams. Everybody affected by it suffered, and many still do to this day, but she did some-

thing about it, and that is her legacy – the fact that she continued to keep going through the pain.

If she had lived long enough, she would have explained individually to every single person in the country what had happened in her son's case. She was on a mission to seek out the truth, pure and simple. Just being able to tell one more person was enough for her some days. It was those small victories that helped her keep plugging away. She'd talk to the lamppost if she thought it would do any good.

John Herbert, Hillsborough survivor

One of the best things about meeting Anne was getting to know so many of the other survivors and we do all look out for each other now. It's an enormous help to know you're not alone. Anne brought people together who can help each other and that's a brilliant legacy.

The families deserve a bit of peace. We're alright, we came home. They need it to be sorted, you can see it in them. 96 died, but there's thousands affected by it.

The fight for justice might have ended years ago, but for Anne. She kept it going on her own, she was the lone voice after everyone else had given in. And she was my mate.

Steve Rotheram, MP

It is all too easy for society to accept titles like 'the Iron Lady' bestowed upon a former Prime Minister, but true unyielding determination isn't a quality confined to politicians on the world stage. Anne Williams was undoubtedly a steely character hewed from the furnace of the campaign for truth and justice.

When people told her to give up, she came back fighting even harder. What those in authority who foolishly believed the Hillsborough campaign would simply fade with the mists of time singularly failed to recognise is the power of a mother's love for her child. When the establishment slammed the doors of justice in her face, she never went away. And when cancer crippled her physically in her dying days, she left no one in any doubt that it was every Hillsborough campaigner's duty to finish the job she had been instrumental in helping to shape.

Whilst Anne undoubtedly mined very deep reserves of personal resolve to continue her fight despite the ravages of her illness, she also took great comfort from the support she continued to receive from ordinary people the length and breadth of the country.

She, in return, gave hope to thousands that the political and legal processes would one day be forced to recognise the full truth and horror of one of the biggest establishment cover-ups in British history.

Whilst Anne's death may have been expected it was no less painful to the family and friends she left behind. Despite the cruel timing of her loss, she thankfully lived long enough to attend the High Court in

December 2012 to hear the Lord Chief Justice pronounce the original verdicts as unsound; quash the accidental death decision of Coroner Dr Stefan Popper in 1989 and announce fresh inquests into the deaths.

Whilst we are grateful for that, Anne will of course miss the culmination of her 24 year campaign and the opportunity to do the one thing she told me she wanted more than anything else − the chance to pick up Kevin's death certificate (which she had steadfastly refused to accept due to its accidental death verdict), to place alongside his birth certificate in a box of memories of Kevin that she had carefully gathered.

Hillsborough continues to be an enormous cross to bear for any of the families or survivors connected to that day. The truth is, many of us will never know the physical, emotional and psychological toll that fighting for what most of us take for granted (natural justice) had on people like Anne.

For many observers in Britain her story is the most well known, as many have long been aware that Kevin was alive far beyond the 3.15pm arbitrary cut off point, and that with a proper emergency plan deployed, he could and should have been saved.

For almost a quarter of a century, the fight for truth and justice became the work of Anne's life. She was routinely let down by an establishment hell-bent on protecting themselves rather than supporting the bereaved, the survivors and a city in shock.

Kevin's last word before he died on the pitch at Hillsborough was 'Mum'. Anne's relentless pursuit of justice for her son personified the unending bond of a mother's unconditional love for her child.

In the end, that's what Anne's legacy is; one of love and unique inspiration.

History will remember her as a mother that wouldn't give up on her child, a campaigner that shook the foundations of the establishment and as an ordinary woman who became an extraordinary campaigner.

Whilst Anne will not be there to fulfil her ultimate wish, she did see the country accept the truth of Hillsborough – and those that are left will continue the fight in her absence until FINALLY, there is justice for the 96.

Spirit of Shankly, Liverpool FC supporters union
For the last 20 odd years of her life, Anne fought for justice. The evidence and truth she fought for is now in the public arena and easily accessible.

It is our responsibility, our promise to Anne, to ensure justice is carried out.

South Yorkshire Police, West Midlands Police, the FA, Duckenfield, Bettison, Beechey – these are names that had tormented Anne for years, names that are now being seen on a daily basis for what they really are and what they did.

These are the names that now need to be brought to

justice and if Anne taught us anything, we must never give up the fight.

When Skies Are Grey, Everton fanzine

Thousands of words of tribute have been written about Anne and we were proud to have known her, even though she referred to us as 'When Skies Are Blue' in her book!

In many ways, it was her tenacity to discover the truth about what happened to her son Kevin that kept Hillsborough on the agenda and helped pave the way for the future justice that she sadly won't be around to see. Anne was a normal Merseyside mum with the type of decency and determination to overcome the odds that typifies our wonderful city.

JFT96.

Tony Barrett, The Times

I first met Anne Williams in the spring of 2002. I had just started a job as a news reporter on the Liverpool Echo and a friend of mine suggested I should interview Anne about her ongoing battle for justice for Kevin.

At the time, Hillsborough was not on the public agenda like it is today and it would be a full decade before the truth revealed itself to the world. Anne, though, had already been battling for 13 years. Indifference to her cause could – and perhaps, given the odds stacked against her, should – have made her give up.

But in the very first interview that I conducted with Anne it became abundantly clear that she would never give in. She never had it in her.

It wasn't just her determined manner or her obvious love for her son, it was the encyclopaedic knowledge she had built up of Hillsborough and its causes. It was the pathologist's eye for detail she had developed about the causes of death and how, in certain circumstances, it may be averted.

For me, a young reporter, it was an education, one that I will never forget. Anne's knowledge didn't just shame those in power who covered up what had happened at Hillsborough, it also embarrassed the industry that I was now part of. If a mum with a family to care for and grief to deal with could unearth so many previously hidden facts, why couldn't an investigative journalist have done the same?

The same thought struck me a decade later as Anne was so spectacularly vindicated by the publication of the Hillsborough Independent Panel report. Again, she went through how Kevin had died and why he should have been saved. Only this time, she did so in the knowledge that everything she had always believed to be true had been proven.

At the subsequent press conference I was able to ask Anne many of the same questions that I had first posed ten years earlier and her answers were still as informed and as passionate as they had been when we first spoke.

Neither the passage of time nor the victory that had belatedly come her way had dimmed her determination to tell the world what had happened to her son.

For that reason – and many others besides – Anne Williams remains the most remarkable individual I have come across.

A tireless campaigner, a self-educated expert on pathology, an ordinary woman who took on the establishment and won and, more than anything, a wonderful mother, she was everything that any of us could ever wish to be and more.

Judith Moritz,
BBC News North of England Correspondent
Anne never trained officially as a solicitor. But to chat to her, you'd imagine that she'd been practising law for years. Sometimes, when interviewing her for the BBC, it was hard to keep up, so detailed was her knowledge of the latest development. It was an expertise which Anne did not acquire out of choice, and it was underpinned by love.

David Conn, The Guardian
It is yet another dimension of the Hillsborough tragedy that Anne Williams died without seeing the new inquest and justice process for which she fought so unceasingly.

Battling on, for her beloved son Kevin, through so

many years when few were listening, finally Anne, with the other Hillsborough families, became recognised not as some Liverpool rabble, but as a shining example: an everyday person, a mother, embodying the extraordinary power and depth of human love.

She was at least there, frail but steadfast, to see the inquest she fought against for 21 years quashed in an hour and a half at the High Court in December 2012. Proved right by the end of her life, she was greatly and widely admired.

Brian Reade, Daily Mirror

I first met Anne 22 years ago when few wanted to know about the travesty of Hillsborough. There was no campaign for justice, indeed little appetite for it.

The families, whose wounds were still raw from the deaths of their loved ones, and the blows rained down on them by the system, felt beaten by the lies and indifference.

Apart from this frail mother of three from Formby.

Anne was determined to get the accidental death verdict on her son Kevin, overturned, and I was trying to get her story into the public domain. It's still one of the most heart-breaking stories I've ever heard.

Last September, the Hillsborough Independent Panel report totally vindicated her battle and the accidental death verdicts were quashed. Weeks later, Anne was diagnosed with terminal cancer, undoubtedly brought on by the stress of a life battling for justice for her son.

I saw her from a distance, in her wheelchair at the 24th anniversary memorial, which she attended against doctor's advice.

Once again I was looking in awe at the phenomenally courageous woman I'd met 22 years previously. One of the bravest, most tenacious people I have ever met. And a mother beyond comparison.

Without her I doubt the families would be in the position they are today, on the brink of justice.

That she died before a new inquest was held, and that she didn't get to see correct words put on Kevin's death certificate, is cruelty beyond belief. It is to the eternal shame of this country, and both Tory and Labour governments, that she didn't. And the perfect reminder of why these families need justice soon. Before another one dies, mostly through the pain of the battle against the wall of lies they've had to butt their head against for almost a quarter of a century.

When the Daily Mirror recently won the Hugh Cudlipp award for its Hillsborough campaign I dedicated it to a Mother's Love. None was stronger than Anne Williams. Not just among the Hillsborough mothers but in the history of motherhood.

Which is not a bad epitaph.

RIP Anne.

It was a beautiful, and unforgettable, privilege to have known you.

Luke Traynor, Daily Mirror

I remember many long phone calls with Anne during which she patiently explained each twist and turn in her tragic story and the constant hurdles placed in her way. Her conviction and sheer honesty always came shining through.

When we chatted at her home just weeks before she died, her optimism, refusal to become bitter and in particular her regular smiles, despite the fact she no doubt knew she did not have long left, were truly admirable. Anne was a woman of grit whose dogged pursuit for what is right remains a wonderful example to us all.

Charlotte Hennessy, HFH member (who lost dad James at Hillsborough)

I was put in contact with Anne five years ago when researching into my father's death. He was also killed at Hillsborough. She was a very kind lady who welcomed me with open arms.

We had only ever chatted via emails at first and she would always take the time to ask if I was ok and how my family was.

As the Hillsborough Panel's work was in full force, our friendship became very close and we attended most meetings together.

Anne always considered others, their feelings, their experience. It didn't matter if you were another family member, survivor, fan, she always had time for everyone even when grieving for the loss of her youngest son, uncovering the shocking truth of his death, and fighting against the system.

Behind the scenes, Anne was a very loving, caring mother, grandmother, sister and aunt. She valued her family and friendships immensely. Everything she did, she did for her family.

She said to me several times 'If I can get Kevin's evidence recognised, it will open the gates for other families'. She always remained focused despite the many setbacks. I find it so distressing that another parent has passed away without seeing those accountable for the loss of their child being brought to justice. 24 years is nearly my entire life, so far. It is unacceptable that we are still waiting. It is unacceptable that a woman who fought so hard did not get to see what she had fought so tirelessly for.

Anne taught me to never give up, no matter how hard the door is slammed, or how distressing the evidence, no matter how vicious the lies, or how many times you have to repeat yourself, never give up.

Anne's death has left a big hole in many people's lives. I miss her little texts, I miss her humour and miss the comfort of her strength. It was a privilege to call her my friend. She was, and always will be, my good egg.

I'm also very proud of Sara and the rest of the family for their continued dignity and strength despite their devastating loss. Anne would be proud of them.

Sammy Irooth, Big Reds Official LFC Supporters Club, Indonesia

Anne was not just a great woman and a fantastic mum, she was also an inspiration for many people. The fact that she fought tirelessly day by day for 24 years to give Kevin and others the justice they all deserved is simply amazing. Few people in this world could have kept going for so long.

What Anne did in her life touched many hearts. The Iron Lady flag is just a little tribute from us to her as a token of our respect. Even though we're many miles away from L4, the fight for justice is always in our minds and has the total support of the Big Reds.

Phil Rowan, HFH campaigner

I met Anne at a fundraiser for Hope For Hillsborough. At the time I was starting to question if we would ever see any justice. I was inspired by Anne and her determination, and knew we had to back her all the way to see justice as she had all the evidence.

We used to speak every month or so on the phone about her campaign and I remember when she told me that she was thinking about withdrawing her e-petition for a debate into Kevin's case as she was a bit embarrassed that it was so far away from the 100,000 necessary with only a few days left.

I told her to leave it with us, and along with Sean O'Reilly-Doyle and other fans groups, we tweeted loads of celebs. It started going mad and we got the names required on the last day. It was amazing how it took off and Anne was made up.

Every time we spoke it was only about Hillsborough. I said to her once, 'Anne one day we will speak, and because we have justice you will just tell me about a holiday or the grandkids'.

I regret that Anne never lived that long, but without doubt, we would not be where we are now without her. She was the bravest person I ever met.

Chris McLoughlin, The Kop Magazine editor

Have you ever seen that cartoon in which an animated escaped convict is trying to hide from the law but no matter where he turns Deputy Droopy is already there waiting for him?

That was Anne Williams. An inspirational, determined lady who was prepared to relentlessly hound those people down who were denying her what she wanted most – justice for her son Kevin – until she got it.

Those responsible for the Hillsborough disaster and those responsible for the subsequent cover-up have tried to hide for 24 years. There have been abuses of power. Playing the system. Barriers put up behind red tape against a backdrop of prejudiced views and deliberate besmirching. But whatever they did, whatever they tried, however they tried to send the campaign for justice off course, Anne would always find another way to keep her fight going. Three times she had her attempts to get the original inquest verdicts quashed. Three times she failed. But she never gave up.

She simply looked for another route. A different legal avenue. Another way of taking the fight to them. European courts, government e-petitions. Whatever it took.

That she has lost her life to cancer before the inquests are re-held is cruel beyond belief, but for her to see the High Court quash those inquest verdicts following the Hillsborough Independent Panel's Report on September 12 was at least something.

She may have been from Formby, but Anne epitomised the 'Liverpool Mums' that Bill Kenwright spoke so movingly of at the Memorial Service shortly before she passed away. That she was there, on the front row of the Kop in a wheelchair, against doctor's expectations, says it all about her indomitable spirit.

Those who spotted her being wheeled into Anfield stood up and applauded. They were clapping a lady of real courage. A lady of dignity. A lady who should never have had to spend the final 24 years of her life fighting for justice. Fighting for accountability. Fighting for Kevin.

That fight now goes on without her, but when it is won – and by God it will be won – then the part Anne played will not be forgotten.

Anne Williams. Rest in peace.

Anne Williams
1951-2013
The Journey To Justice

6 February, 1951: Anne is born at Watchard Lane, Formby to mum Margaret and dad Eddie

July 1966: Anne leaves school and starts secretarial work in Formby

August 1970: Anne marries first husband

July 24, 1971: Anne's first son Michael is born

May 27, 1973: Anne's second son Kevin is born

Autumn, 1975: Anne divorces first husband on grounds of cruelty

1977: Anne marries Steve Williams

July 6, 1979: Anne's daughter Sara is born

April 11, 1981: 38 Tottenham Hotspur supporters suffer crush injuries during the FA Cup semi-final match against Wolverhampton Wanderers at Hillsborough. Fans are pulled out of the Leppings Lane end enclosure by police officers and moved to the other end of the ground. The FA consequently moves FA Cup semi-finals away from Hillsborough for six years. Recommendations are made to improve safety but these are never carried out.

April 12, 1987: Hillsborough hosts its first FA Cup semi-final – Leeds v Coventry – for six years. Despite having considerably more fans travelling to the game, Leeds are allocated the Leppings Lane end as South Yorkshire Police's policy is to give fans travelling from the south the Kop end, irrespective of numbers.

April 9, 1988: Liverpool beat Nottingham Forest 2-1 in the FA Cup semi-final at Hillsborough. Despite a considerably larger average attendance, LFC are allocated the smaller Leppings Lane end despite a protest from chief executive Peter Robinson. Many Reds fans complain after the game of over-crowding, particularly in the two central pens behind the goal.

March 20, 1989: Liverpool are again drawn to play Nottingham Forest in the FA Cup semi-final and the FA again choose Hillsborough as the venue. Peter

Robinson appeals about the ticket allocation again, this time pointing out the over-crowding in the Leppings Lane end the previous season, but the request is again refused.

April 14, 1989: 15-year-old Kevin Williams ask if he can go with his mates to watch his beloved Reds at Hillsborough. Parents Anne and Steve say no at first but change their minds after considering how hard he is working at school, much to Kevin's delight.

April 15, 1989:

7am – Anne sees Kevin off as he sets out for Sheffield, telling him to enjoy himself but to be careful. Kevin responds with a cheery wave and says, "No worries, Mum. Three-nil!".

1.30pm – Kevin and friend Andy Duncan enter the stadium at Hillsborough via the Leppings Lane end turnstiles. They go into Pen 4 at first but move into Pen 3 shortly afterwards for a better view. They lie down on the virtually empty terrace and enjoy the spring sunshine.

2.30pm – Roadworks along the route to Sheffield cause delays to those travelling across the Pennines and a build-up of supporters trying to gain entry through the bottleneck area that permits access to the Leppings Lane end starts to cause congestion outside the ground. As well as the 10,100 spectators with terrace tickets, Reds fans with tickets for the seated upper tier and adjacent West Stand must also enter through this end of the stadium meaning the 23 turnstiles there must process all 24,256 Liverpool fans in attendance. The previous year, Match Commander Chief Inspector Brian Mole had implemented barricades across the road leading to the Leppings Lane turnstiles to monitor access to the cramped entrance area. Mole however was taken off the 1989 match three weeks beforehand and replaced by Chief Inspector David Duckenfield, who had no experience of managing a football game of this size and did not implement any monitoring system outside.

2.40pm – As the situation outside the ground worsens, a request is sent to Police Control to send spare mounted officers to the Leppings Lane end while an announcement is made over the tannoy asking people on the terraces at that end to move forward as the central pens are already nearly full. PC Buxton radios through to suggest delaying the kick-off as happened at the 1987 semi-final between Coventry and Leeds but this request is denied by Duckenfield and second-in-command Superintendent Bernard Murray, who have access to five TV screens in their control room overlooking the Leppings Lane terrace which show live images from fully-functional CCTV cameras complete with zoom capability. Despite the central two of the five pens which divide the terrace being clearly close to capacity, still no attempt is made to prevent access to the tunnel that leads into them or to steer people into the emptier adjacent ones.

2.52pm – Superintendent Marshall on duty in the area around the Leppings Lane terrace entrance radios Duckenfield to tell him people may be killed outside the ground if gates are not opened to relieve the pressure. Duckenfield admits later that he 'froze' – he then gives the order to open Gate C, allowing 2,000 people to stream into the ground. Many head straight down the unblocked tunnel directly in front of them which leads into the already-packed central pens. With an estimated 3,000 people now in the central pens - almost double its official capacity – a severe crush develops within them, with the fences at the front and the side of each pen preventing any escape. Survivor Eddie Spearitt describes it as "like being in a vice, getting tighter and tighter".

3pm – The match kicks off with many in the ground unaware that people are dying behind one of the goals. Constable Waugh from South Yorkshire Police HQ calls through asking if ambulances are required but is told by the Control Room to remain on stand-by. Police Control do however request more officers and dog handlers as they believe a pitch invasion is taking place with supporters beginning to climb over the perimeter fence to escape the crush.

3.04pm – Liverpool's Peter Beardsley hits the crossbar at the other end of the field leading to an inevitable surge in the pens and a minute later a crush barrier in pen 3 gives way, causing supporters to fall to the ground.

3.06pm – Superintendent Roger Greenwood goes onto the pitch and instructs referee Ray Lewis from Great Bookham to halt the match and take the players from the field. After initially closing gates at the front of the pens that had sprung open due to the pressure inside and pushing back in fans trying to climb over the perimeter fencing, police officers finally do open the gates and begin trying to get people out. Supporters from the upper tier begin to pull those in the lower up to safety while Murray radios for a fleet of ambulances.

3.13pm – A St John's ambulance enters the pitch and positions itself by pens 3 and 4 – 44 ambulances begin to arrive, but they are told that fans are fighting and only one more makes it onto the pitch. There is no call for doctors or nurses over the PA until 3.30pm.

3.17pm – FA chief executive Graham Kelly visits the Police Control Room where he is told by Duckenfield that there had been an inrush of fans after they had forced open Gate C. He later admits this to be untrue but by 3.40pm, BBC Radio Two broadcasts, "unconfirmed reports are that a door was broken at the end that was holding Liverpool supporters".

3.28pm – Kevin Williams is pulled out of pen 3 by PC Michael Craighill, who tries unsuccessfully to resuscitate him and leaves him on the pitch.

3.30pm – Kevin is spotted by Stevie Hart, who with assistance from fellow supporter Tony O'Keefe and two police officers loads him onto an advertising hoarding being used as a makeshift stretcher and carries him to the other end of the pitch, where they leave him in the care of a police officer who swears at them before walking off.

3.32pm – Kevin is spotted moving on the ground by off-duty Merseyside policeman Derek Bruder who comes down from his position in the stands and, after finding a pulse, tries to revive him.

3.37pm – An ambulance drives past Bruder on the pitch, which he tries unsuccessfully to flag down. This is the ambulance driven by Tony Edwards whose existence was denied by official sources until proven by video evidence found by the Cook Report five years later. Shortly afterward a female St John's Ambulance worker pushes Bruder aside and takes over resuscitation only to declare, "He's gone".

3.45pm – Special WPC Debra Martin carries Kevin to the Hillsborough gymnasium with the help of another police officer. She also finds a weak pulse and tries to revive him.

4pm – Kevin opens his eyes and says, "Mum", before dying in Debra Martin's arms.

4.06pm – Kevin is pronounced dead by Dr Curpen. The horrific toll begins to emerge from the day's events: 730 supporters injured and ultimately 96 fatalities (Tony Bland's life-support machine was turned off in 1993), with only 14 of them ever making it to a hospital despite 44 ambulances with 84 trained personnel being within 300 yards of the disaster scene.

April 16, 1989: Anne and Steve Williams travel to Sheffield to identify Kevin's body. Liverpool FC open the gates at Anfield to allow the bereaved, supporters and the general public to pay their respects to those who have lost their lives. That evening a memorial service is held at the city's Roman Catholic cathedral and the following day Lord Justice Taylor is appointed to conduct a public inquiry into the disaster, with the West Midlands Police force later instructed to examine the role of their South Yorkshire counterparts.

April 19, 1989: The Sun newspaper, on the instructions of editor Kelvin MacKenzie, publishes a front page story under the headline, 'The Truth', claiming that Liverpool supporters stole from victims as they lay dead, urinated on the police and attacked officers, firemen and ambulance crews during the rescue operation. Various media outlets report similar allegations, which come from comments made by Sheffield Hallam Conservative MP Irvine Patnick and unnamed police sources. Fury erupts on Merseyside. Copies of the paper are burned and a boycott is started, which still stands today. Two days after The Sun's story, Home Secretary Douglas Hurd says in the House of Commons that 19 police officers were physically assaulted at the ground and that South Yorkshire Police are gathering information to pass on to the inquiry. On May 3 however he is unable to state how these injuries were sustained and no evidence is ever passed on to the inquiry. The lack of a single witness statement, piece of evidence or image frame from the thousands of press photographs and 71 hours of recorded video footage leads Lord Taylor to completely dismiss the allegations in his report.

April 21, 1989: After a funeral service at Our Lady of Compassion Church in Formby, Kevin is cremated with his ashes later scattered at Anfield.

April 22, 1989: With Anfield now a shrine as half the pitch and much of the Kop are covered with tributes, a mile of scarves across Stanley Park links Goodison and Anfield as a symbol of the unity felt across Merseyside before a service at Liverpool's ground to mark a week since the tragedy.

April 29, 1989: A memorial service takes place at the city's Anglican Cathedral and the following day Liverpool play their first game since the disaster when they travel to Glasgow to take on Celtic in a friendly to raise funds for the victims of Hillsborough.

May 3, 1989: The Reds return to competitive action at Goodison in a rescheduled league game against Everton while the following Sunday, May 7, Liverpool beat Nottingham Forest in the replayed semi-final at Old Trafford, Manchester to set up a fitting all-Merseyside FA Cup final against their neighbours, who had beaten Norwich City at Villa Park on April 15.

May 20, 1989: On the same day Liverpool beat Everton 3-2 after extra time in an emotional FA Cup Final and dedicate their victory to the 96, a new version of

Gerry Marsden's 'Ferry Cross The Mersey' is released
to raise funds for the Hillsborough families. It features
Marsden, Paul McCartney, Holly Johnson and the
Christians, reaching number one in the charts for three
weeks.

August 1, 1989: Lord Justice Taylor publishes his interim report into the disaster after the submission of
3,776 written statements of evidence, 1,550 letters, 71
hours of video footage and the oral evidence of 174
witnesses. Taylor finds the main reason for the disaster
to be the failure of police control. Liverpool supporters are fully exonerated from the stream of accusations
hurled in their direction and are praised for their efforts in supporting the rescue operation.

The slow reaction of police to initiate the Disaster
Plan, the Football Association, Sheffield City Council
and Sheffield Wednesday Football Club (the ground
did not have a valid safety certificate) are all criticised
in the report but the most scathing verdict is reserved
for Match Commander David Duckenfield.

His decision to open Gate C and failure to guide fans
away from the packed central plans are described as
'blunders of the first magnitude' while he is also con-
demned for his failure to take effective control and
South Yorkshire Police's attempts to blame supporters
for being late and drunk. He is immediately suspended
from duty.

November 30, 1989: South Yorkshire Chief Constable Peter Wright, and his Police Authority, offer an out-of-court damages settlement to the bereaved and injured following civil proceedings taken against them. The offer carries no acceptance of liability. It is estimated compensation costs could amount to a total of £50 million.

January 1990: The Taylor inquiry publishes its final report concluding that South Yorkshire Police, led by Duckenfield and Superintendent Bernard Murray, 'fundamentally lost control' of the situation and makes a total of 76 recommendations, the most significant being the introduction of all-seater stadiums.

April 18, 1990: Three days after the permanent Anfield memorial and eternal flame are unveiled on the first anniversary of Hillsborough, South Yorkshire Coroner Dr Stefan Popper begins the process of inquests despite the Director of Public Prosecutions not having yet decided whether to press any criminal charges, as is the normal procedure. A series of mini-inquests take place at a rate of around eight per day. Details of every victim – including the blood-alcohol level, even in the many cases where it was negative – are read out to the jury by members of the West Midlands Police force, who are again charged with providing evidence, with no cross-examination allowed.

May 2, 1990: Anne and Steve Williams travel to Sheffield for Kevin's mini-inquest. Shortly before entering the court, they are informed that Kevin had called for his mother before dying in the arms of WPC Debra Martin at 4pm. Her evidence is played down in court with pathologist Dr David Slater telling the coroner Kevin's injuries were amongst the worst of all the victims and would have made it impossible for him to have spoken. PC Derek Bruder's evidence about Kevin's 'convulsions' is also presented in a manner supporting the view that he was beyond saving.

May 3, 1990: DI Matt Sawers from West Midlands Police visits PC Bruder at his Liverpool home to clarify certain aspects of his evidence. Bruder is challenged over the convulsions he saw, the pulse he found and the ambulance he tried to flag down. After hours of discussion, Sawers rings pathologist David Slater who also questions Bruder over his evidence. Bruder signs a new statement conceding the medical possibility that he could have been mistaken over the pulse and changes the 'convulsion' he saw from the stands to a 'twitch' but is adamant about the existence of the ambulance at 3.37. Sawers then visits Anne and Steve Williams at their home in Formby to inform them of Bruder's changed statement and also tells them there will be a second inquest into Kevin's death the following day which they don't need to attend.

May 4, 1990: PC Bruder's second statement is read out at Kevin's second mini-inquest to reinforce the pathologist's view that he could not have been saved nor have spoken the word 'Mum'. Bruder later makes a formal complaint that his evidence was not presented in its entirety or in a professional manner. Neither Bruder or WPC Martin, who also made two statements, were invited to give evidence in person at either inquest.

August 30, 1990: The Director of Public Prosecutions decides there 'is no evidence to justify any criminal proceedings' against South Yorkshire Police, Sheffield Wednesday FC, Sheffield City Council of the safety engineers. He also states there is 'insufficient evidence to justify proceedings against any officer of the South Yorkshire Police or any other person for any offence'.

October, 1990: South Yorkshire Police launch a civil action against Sheffield Wednesday and its engineers, Eastwood and partners, to try and reclaim part of the costs of their out-of-court settlement.

November 19, 1990: The main inquest into the Hillsborough disaster opens at Sheffield Town Hall but immediately there is controversy as Dr Popper decides no evidence would be heard concerning events after 3.15pm on the day of the disaster. He says this is because 'traumatic asphyxia' was the 'sole cause' of every death and 3.15pm would have been 'the latest time when the real damage was done'. The controversial decision is made despite evidence showing not all the victims were dead by 3.15pm and is in effect saying that those died or survived did so irrespective of medical treatment as the first ambulance only arrived on the pitch at 3.15pm.

March 28, 1991: The inquest closes with a jury reaching a nine-to-two majority verdict that all who died at Hillsborough did so as a result of 'accidental death'. The verdict is met with dismay and anger by the families. Confused by the differing accounts she has been given of her son's last minutes, Anne Williams attends a meeting of the Hillsborough Family Support Group and begins working with Sheila Coleman and Ann Adlington to discover what really happened to Kevin.

July 11, 1991: The Police Complaints Authority, after receiving 17 complaints from members of the public, instructs South Yorkshire Police to commence disciplinary proceedings against Duckenfield and Bernard Murray. Duckenfield faces four charges of neglect of duty and one of discreditable conduct while Murray faces one charge of neglect of duty

September, 1991: Anne receives the transcripts of Kevin's two mini-inquests and discovers that both

Bruder and Martin had found a pulse after 3.15. Neither DS Killoch or DI Sawers had previously informed her of this information.

November 5, 1991: Anne and five other families meet with Edward Fitzgerald QC who agrees to take their cases on and promises to explore legal avenues to obtain new inquests.

November 10, 1991: David Duckenfield takes early retirement on medical grounds, thus avoiding the disciplinary hearing.

December 15, 1991: Anne meets Derek Bruder at Hope Street police station in Liverpool and hears first-hand how he tried to save Kevin. He declines to make a further statement but promises to give evidence should there be new inquests.

January 13, 1992: Following judicial advice, the Police Complaint Authority decides not to proceed against Murray as it was a 'joint-charge'.

February 22, 1992: Anne meets Debra Martin and learns first-hand about her son's final moments. WPC Martin says how she was pressured by West Midlands Police into making a second statement omitting any signs of life she found in Kevin, which she signed without reading. She makes a third statement reiterating the contents her first one, witnessed and signed by solicitor Ann Adlington.

April 15, 1992: Having compiled medical reports to support their evidence from consultant forensic pathologists Dr Ian West and Dr James Burns, Anne and the other five families issue a memorial to the Attorney General under Section 13 of the 1988 Coroners Act requesting new inquests. It is turned down as being "not in the interests of justice".

April 6, 1993: The six bereaved families are granted applications for a judicial review of the inquest verdicts.

November 5, 1993: After a week long judicial review hearing at the High Court in London, Lord Justice McCowan and Mr Justice Turner rule in favour of the coroner over the six families following detailed submissions.

June 2, 1994: An edition of The Cook Report called *'Kevin's mum'* features Anne and her battle to find out the truth about Hillsborough. Through the programme's research, she is further able to build up her body of evidence through survivors Stevie Hart and Tony O'Keefe, ambulance driver Tony Edwards, and police corruption victim George Tomkins.

November 26,1994: Anne's MP Sir Malcolm Thornton secures a parliamentary debate in the House of Commons into Kevin's death. Attorney General Sir Nicholas Lyell says he will consider the evidence found by the Cook Report if submitted with a new memorial.

July, 1995: Anne separates from Steve Williams.

November, 1995: No Last Rights, Professor Phil Scraton's 375-page analysis of the legal proceedings and media coverage of Hillsborough, is published. Despite highlighting the gross injustice suffered by the bereaved families and making 87 detailed recommendations for institutional reform, only three national newspapers bother to give the fresh development any press coverage.

March, 1996: Anne's second memorial to the Attorney General requesting a new inquest into Kevin's death is rejected as being "not in the interests of justice."

December 5, 1996: Jimmy McGovern's drama-documentary 'Hillsborough' airs on television and leads to calls for the inquests to be reopened.

December 17, 1996: Merseyside Labour MP Peter Kilfoyle tells the House of Commons there should be a new investigation into the tragedy. Home Secretary

Michael Howard responds stating his commitment to "searching for the truth" but says "he would not take a decision to reopen the inquiry lightly."

May 1, 1997: The Labour Party, having campaigned on Merseyside with a promise of a new inquiry into Hillsborough, wins the general election by a massive landslide.

May 3, 1997: The Football Supporters Association organises a 'red card' protest at the Liverpool v Tottenham game, which is live on Sky Sports. Before kick-off at Anfield, players and over 40,000 supporters hold up red cards with the words 'Justice for the 96' printed on them.

May 10, 1997: The Hillsborough Justice Concert is held at Anfield to raise funds for the justice campaign. The Manic Street Preachers, Stereophonics, Lightning Seeds, Dodgy, Beautiful South, Space, Bootleg Beatles, Smaller, Holly Johnston and the London Gospel Choir are amongst the artists to perform in front of 34,000. A CD of the concert is later released by Virgin.

May 11, 1997: Liverpool visit Sheffield Wednesday on the final day of the season but supporters trying to enter the ground have floral tributes and justice banners confiscated by South Yorkshire Police.

June 30, 1997: Over 40 bereaved families travel to Westminster to meet new Home Secretary Jack Straw whose responsibility the Hillsborough issue has now become. He tells them there will be an independent judicial scrutiny into the disaster, conducted by Appeal Court judge Lord Justice Stuart-Smith.

October 6, 1997: As part of the independent scrutiny, Lord Justice Stuart-Smith visits Liverpool to meet with the families at Liverpool's Maritime Museum. Some are delayed by parking problems, prompting the judge to quip to the Hillsborough Family Support Group's Phil Hammond: "have you got a few of your people or are they like the Liverpool fans turning up at the last minute." They are his first words to the families, who are understandably outraged.

Early 1998: With compensation claims still ongoing it is revealed that there have been 36 settlements for loss of financial dependency, 50 fatal claims and 1,035 personal injury claims with a total of £13.5 million paid in compensation and legal costs. This is far less than the original estimate that was in the region of £50million.

February 14, 1998: Liverpool travel to Sheffield Wednesday and again supporters have flowers taken from them by South Yorkshire Police. The game is also sponsored by The Sun, much to the Liverpool fans' bewilderment.

February 18, 1998: The families travel to Westminster again to meet with Jack Straw before the announcement of Stuart-Smith's verdict. He tells them there will be no further review. In the wake of the announcement the Hillsborough Justice Campaign, a breakaway group from the Hillsborough Family Support Group, is formed to continue the fight for justice using different tactics. Survivors of the disaster and supporters are allowed to join whereas the Hillsborough Family Support Group is made up only of the bereaved families.

April, 1998: Original and amended statements by South Yorkshire Police officers after Hillsborough are made available by the Home Office. It confirms there has been a huge cover-up.

August 20, 1998: With a private prosecution under way, Duckenfield and Murray appear in Leeds Magistrates Court to hear a range of charges, including manslaughter, read against them. They respond by claiming they cannot be given a fair trial given the subsequent media coverage.

October, 1998: There is outrage after Norman Bettison is appointed as Chief Constable of Merseyside

Police. Bettison was part of the South Yorkshire Police's information team for the Hillsborough inquiry, responsible for gathering and amending statements.

Autumn, 1998: The Hillsborough Justice Campaign announce they are organising a boycott of the Sheffield Wednesday v Liverpool match due to be played at Hillsborough on May 8, 1999, following the treatment of Liverpool fans in recent visits to Sheffield. The Hillsborough Family Support Group disagrees with the action, highlighting the differences between the two groups.

February 11, 1999: The Director of Public Prosecutions rejects a request by Duckenfield and Murray to intervene and discontinue the prosecution against them.

February, 1999: In what appears to be an attempt to avoid the planned HJC boycott, Sheffield Wednesday announce they will finally erect a memorial at Hillsborough. The HJC say the boycott is still on.

March 25, 1999: Anne's book, *When You Walk Through The Storm,* is published telling the story of the evidence she uncovered and her fight for justice. She becomes active within the Hillsborough Justice Campaign and later becomes chairman.

April, 1999: Barnes Travel, the firm that takes more coaches to Liverpool away games than any other, announces they will not be running any coaches to Hillsborough for the proposed boycott the following month.

April 15, 1999: Hillsborough Family Support Group chairman Trevor Hicks makes a plea for justice for the 96 at the 10th anniversary service at Anfield. Around 10,000 people attend.

May 8, 1999: The Hillsborough Justice Campaign hold a rally on the steps of St George's Hall while Sheffield Wednesday are playing Liverpool at Hillsborough. Of 7,500 tickets allocated to the club, only 1,062 are sold, making the boycott a success. Some of the Liverpool fans who do travel to Hillsborough lay flowers next to the new memorial while Sheffield Wednesday place 96 red roses on front row seats of the Leppings Lane end and a minute's silence and prayers are held before kick-off.

July, 1999: Duckenfield and Murray are committed for trial by a Leeds stipendiary magistrate, despite an application by the pair to abort the case against them.

January 2000: Eileen McBride, a nurse who was in the upper tier of the Leppings Lane on the day of the disaster and administered first aid on the pitch, wins damages against South Yorkshire Police for the effect the disaster had on her.

February 16, 2000: Mr Justice Hooper rules that Duckenfield and Murray can be given a fair trial but rules that the defendants 'will not immediately lose their liberty' if convicted.

June 6, 2000: David Duckenfield and Bernard Murray go on trial at Leeds Crown Court.

July 17, 2000: Mr Justice Hooper summises the trial to the jury but his direction on the issue of gross negligence with regard to manslaughter raises concerns with the prosecution.

July 20, 2000: After over 21 hours deliberation, the jury agrees on a majority verdict of 'not guilty' against Bernard Murray.

July 24, 2000: After failing to reach a verdict on David Duckenfield, the jury is discharged.

July 26, 2000: Alun Jones, on behalf of the families, applies for a retrial of Duckenfield with a different judge, arguing that Mr Justice Hooper had wrongly directed the jury. However, Mr Justice Hooper refuses the application, saying that Duckenfield can no longer have a fair trial as a result of all the media coverage.

August 19, 2000: Liverpool supporters attend a rally in Stanley Park before the Reds' first home game of the 2000/2001 season to show support for the Hillsborough Family Support Group and Hillsborough Justice Campaign.

October 10, 2000: Anne's first grandchild, Lena, is born to daughter Sara.

March 2, 2001: Former Police officer Martin Long is awarded an out-of-court compensation settlement of around £330,000 from South Yorkshire Police after claiming to be suffering from late-onset post-traumatic stress. Phil Hammond, who lost his 14-year-old son Philip at Hillsborough, reveals he got £3,500.

July 3, 2004: News breaks that Everton's teenage striker Wayne Rooney has sold his life story to The Sun. Supporters of both Liverpool and Everton react angrily.

July 5, 2004: The Sun prints the first part of Rooney's life-story.

July 7, 2004: In response to angry criticism of Rooney, The Sun prints a full-page apology for its coverage of the Hillsborough disaster. It tries to pin the blame for anger at Rooney on the Liverpool ECHO and Daily Post, who are owned by The Mirror Group, arousing suspicion that the apology is simply to try and recover some of the estimated 50,000 sales-per-day they have lost as a result of their coverage.

July, 2004: Sun managing editor Graham Dudman travels to Merseyside to meet four of the bereaved families to appeal for forgiveness. He offers to campaign for justice on their behalf but only if the Hillsborough Family Support Group accepts The Sun's apology.

August, 2004: Dudman returns to Liverpool to wait in a hotel room while the Hillsborough Family Support Group meets to discuss his offer. They vote to refuse to see him, rejecting The Sun's apology.

May 25, 2005: Steven Gerrard lifts the European Cup in Istanbul wearing a red Hillsborough wristband.

February 28, 2006: Having had a third memorial to the Attorney General rejected, Anne leaves the Hillsborough Justice Campaign. Soon afterwards, she submits Kevin's case to the European Courts of Human Rights under section 2, "The Right To Life".

November 30, 2006: Kelvin MacKenzie tells a group

of businessmen at a lunch in Newcastle that "I wasn't sorry then and I'm not sorry now because we told the truth," regarding The Sun's Hillsborough coverage. It emerges that MacKenzie has been commissioned to present a two-hour radio programme on the BBC, sparking protests from supporters who flood the corporation with complaints.

January 6, 2007: New Liverpool supporters group 'Reclaim The Kop' holds a 'Truth Day' protest at Anfield to coincide with the BBC screening the club's FA Cup third round game against Arsenal. 'THE TRUTH' is held up as a mosaic on The Kop for the first six minutes of the game alongside incessant chanting of 'Justice for the 96'.

April 18, 2008: Anne's second grandchild, Grace, is born to son Michael

Summer, 2008: Anne launches her Hope For Hillsborough group

September 12, 2008: Anne's third grandchild, Finlay, is born to daughter Sara

February 18, 2009: It is revealed that the city of Liverpool will hold a two-minute silence at 3.06pm on April 15 to mark the 20th anniversary of Hillsborough, with the bells from both of the city's Cathedrals to be rung out.

March 30, 2009: Anne's application to the European Court of Human Rights is rejected for being "out of time."

April 15, 2009: Addressing the 20th anniversary memorial service at Anfield which is attended by around 30,000 people – more than double the previous record attendance for the 10th anniversary service – Culture Secretary Andy Burnham is left in no doubt as to the depth of feeling that still exists over the disaster as the crowd interrupts his address with an impassioned plea for 'Justice for the 96'. Burnham, along with Garston and Halewood MP Maria Eagle, call for full disclosure of all Hillsborough documents, which are not due to be released for another decade under the 30-year rule.

June 20, 2009: 4,000 people including families and survivors march on Downing Street to deliver a petition containing over 40,000 signatures demanding a further investigation into the disaster.

July, 2009: The Home Office announces its commitment to release all information not previously made available and its intention to appoint an Independent Panel to oversee the release of the information.

January 26 2010: The members of the Independent Panel are revealed. It is to be chaired by James Jones, the Bishop of Liverpool, and consists of Phil Scraton, professor of criminology at Queen's University, Belfast, and author of Hillsborough: The Truth; Katy Jones, TV and factual producer on Jimmy McGovern's Hillsborough; broadcaster Peter Sissons; Department of Health Associate Chief Medical Officer Dr Bill Kirkup ; human rights lawyer Raju Bhatt; information expert Christine Gifford; investigative journalist Katy Jones; former Northern Ireland Deputy Chief Constable Paul Leighton and former National Archives Chief Executive Sarah Tyacke.

August, 2011: The government appeals the Information Commissioner's decision to make public Hillsborough documents relating to Margaret Thatcher. Within days an online e-petition set up by LFC fan Brian Irvine takes place calling for full disclosure of the hidden documents which soon gains the 100,000 signatures needed to for it to be considered for a parliamentary debate.

October 17, 2011: The debate takes place in the House of Commons and Home Secretary Theresa May confirms, without the need for a vote, that all documents will be released in full to the Independent Panel. For more than four hours, Merseyside MPs and those from further afield detail the particulars of the case and the litany of slurs, insinuations and knock-backs those campaigning for justice have been forced to deal with for so long. Families and campaigners express cautious optimism that finally the truth may start to emerge with the publication of the Indepen-dent Panel's report. In an emotional speech, Liverpool Walton MP Steve Rotheram ends by reading out the names of the 96 so they are recorded for posterity in Hansard.

February 22, 2012: In a Westminster Hall debate into Kevin's case sparked by an e-petition started by Anne that gained over 118,000 signatures, Attorney General Dominic Grieve tells MPs he expects the Independent Panel to unearth further evidence which could tip the balance in Kevin's case – but that no decision could be made until the Panel delivers its report.

September 12, 2012: The long-awaited publication of the Independent Panel's report confirms the truth known on Merseyside for so long:

– Liverpool fans neither caused nor contributed to the deaths of the 96 men, women and children

– A swifter, more appropriate, better focused and prop-erly-equipped response had the potential to save lives

– A contrived, manipulated, vengeful and spiteful attempt to divert the blame onto the fans was undertaken by South Yorkshire Police

Families and survivors are presented with the report and have the opportunity to quiz the Panel about their findings. The most shocking revelations detail how:

– 41 out of the 96 victims could have been saved with a more effective emergency response

– Victims, including children, were checked against police computers for criminal convictions if their blood-alcohol tests came back negative

– Margaret Thatcher expressed her concern that the "broad thrust" of the report constituted a "devastating" criticism of the police

– At a South Yorkshire Police Federation lunch on the same day The Sun's 'The Truth' story appeared, chief constable Peter Wright and secretary Paul Middup stressed the importance of getting the force's 'message' across, namely 'if anybody should be blamed, it should be the drunken ticketless individuals'.

In advance of the Panel's report being publicly released, Prime Minister David Cameron offers a 'profound apology for the double injustice left uncorrected for so long'. A series of apologies began to flood in from the Football Association, Sheffield Wednesday Football Club, Kelvin MacKenzie and Irvine Patnick amongst others, while families, survivors and campaigners express their gratitude to the Panel for their work and relief that their long battle for the truth had been vindicated whilst making plans to continue their quest for justice. A vigil is held later that evening at St George's Hall in memory of the 96 as Liverpool begins to digest one of the most momentous days in the city's history.

September 17, 2012: Anne meets with her legal team to finalise her fourth memorial for a new inquest to the Attorney General.

October 12, 2012: The Independent Police Complaints Commission declares its intention to launch the biggest ever investigation into police in the UK, centred on officers' conduct during and after the disaster, while the Director of Public Prosecutions Keir Starmer also confirms he will also review all fresh evidence – especially from the Hillsborough Independent Panel report – to decide whether individuals or organisations who potentially acted criminally should be prosecuted.

October 16, 2012: Attorney General Dominic Grieve confirms his intention to have the original Hillsborough inquest versions quashed so new ones can be held. Grieve said his consideration of the evidence was far from over, but given the anxiety further delay may cause the families, he was taking the exceptional step of indicating he would apply for new inquests to be held on the basis of the evidence he had already read.

October 22, 2012: A year and a week after the Westminster debate triggered by the e-petition calling for the unredacted release of all Hillsborough documents, families and supporters again travel to London to hear the Commons discuss issues raised by the Independent Panel's report.

As it emerges the names of 1,444 former and serving police officers have been passed on to the IPCC by South Yorkshire Police, Home Secretary Theresa May says she "remained committed to ensuring it has all the resources and powers it needs to carry out its investigations thoroughly, transparently and exhaustively" and confirms there will be cross-party co-operation to see if new laws are needed to compel former officers to co-operate.

Garston and Halewood MP Maria Eagle uses parliamentary privilege to unveil witness evidence that West Yorkshire's Chief Constable, Sir Norman Bettison, an officer for the South Yorkshire force at the time, had bragged of his attempts to "fit-up" Liverpool football supporters after the disaster to John Barry, a Liverpool fan who had been at Hillsborough, when they studied together on a part-time course at Sheffield Business School.

October 24, 2012: Ahead of a West Yorkshire Police special committee meeting which was expected to suspend him, Norman Bettison resigns from his post with immediate effect rather than taking his planned retirement in March 2013.

He continues to deny any wrongdoing but says the continuing scandal had become a distraction from doing his job while the Independent Police Complaints Commission says its investigation into Mr Bettison's role in the aftermath of Hillsborough will still continue. Days later, it is confirmed the Merseyside police authority will begin paying Bettison's £83,000 a year pension despite him still being the subject of two IPCC investigations.

October 26, 2012: Anne confirms she is suffering from terminal cancer. Within days, supporters set up an e-petition calling for Kevin's new inquest to be moved forward and within a matter of weeks it gains the 100,000 signatures needed to potentially trigger a Commons debate. However, the Attorney General says it is not within his power to separate her case from the others.

December 19, 2012: A landmark day in a momentous year as the original accidental death verdicts of the 96 victims are quashed at the High Court with new inquests ordered. The Lord Chief Justice Lord Igor Judge says the new evidence unearthed by the Hillsborough Independent Panel meant it is "inevitable" the verdicts should be quashed while the Government confirms they will cover the costs of the new inquests. The news comes on the same day a new criminal investigation into the Hillsborough Disaster is announced. Confirming the fresh inquiry into the FA Cup semi final which claimed the lives of 96 Liverpool fans on April 15, 1989, Home Secretary Theresa May says it would investigate "all of the people and organisations involved – before, on, and after" the tragedy.

December 23, 2012: Just nine weeks after inception, the Justice Collective's cover of The Hollies' *'He Ain't Heavy, He's My Brother'* is confirmed as the UK Christmas number one seeing off the challenge of X Factor winner James Arthur with sales topping 269,000.

February 13, 2013: As Home Secretary Theresa May announces the expansion of the IPCC to deal with all serious complaints against the police, High Court judge Lord Goldring – a top legal figure in the country – is nominated by the Judicial Office to conduct the new inquests into the 96.

February 18, 2013: Director of Public Prosecutions Keir Starmer tells how prosecutors have established a unique set of arrangements and have broken their usual mould for big investigations because of the length of time families have had to wait for justice over Hillsborough and confirms he requested an early meeting with the coroner to ensure the inquests and investigations can proceed concurrently.

April 14, 2013: A day before the 24th anniversary, Liverpool's first permanent city centre tribute to the Hillsborough 96 is unveiled. The 7ft bronze drum-shaped monument on Old Haymarket, created by local sculptor Tom Murphy, was commissioned by the Hillsborough Justice Campaign and includes a poem written by Daily Post and Echo journalist David Charters.

> *And so, as one, the hushed crowd turned the pages of*
> *the book that held the names of the dead*
> *And the sound that rose from them was like a great*
> *flapping of birds' wings*
> *Into the dark sky and beyond, it carried the memories*
> *of those who had gone – the teachers whose wisdom*
> *was lost, the parents who will never cradle children,*
> *the makers whose hands were stilled, the jokers whose*
> *laughter vanished, the singers whose songs are silence,*
> *the lovers whose love lasts forever...*

April 15, 2013: Families, survivors and supporters gather at Anfield for the first annual memorial service since the truth about Hillsborough was finally confirmed in the previous year's report from the Independent Panel. With her condition rapidly deteriorating, Anne confounds doctors' expectations to attend the service and calls for the fight for justice to continue.

April 18, 2013: Anne passes away peacefully at home with her brother Danny at her side.